HIGHLIGHTS

OF THE COLLECTION

NATIONAL GALLERY of IRELAND

SCALA ARTS & HERITAGE PUBLISHERS

CONTENTS

INTRODUCTION

Niamh MacNally

The National Gallery of Ireland, founded in 1854, houses an impressive collection of over 15,000 artworks. Spanning the history of western European art, from around 1300 to the present day, the collection includes well-known artists, from Mantegna and Titian to Monet and Picasso. Incorporating the various schools and eras, and presented by way of a loose chronology, this guide highlights a selection of the most important works in the collection.

In the early years, judicious purchases included panel paintings by several Early Renaissance masters such as Uccello, Fra Angelico and Granacci, along with fine portraits by Moroni and Fontana. Other notable early acquisitions, which remain collection favourites, include works by Rembrandt, Steen, Poussin, Reynolds and Danby.

Over the past 150 years, the Gallery's collection has been augmented by a series of munificent gifts. In 1902 Countess Milltown donated the contents of her home Russborough, County Wicklow, in memory of her late husband the 6th Earl of Milltown. Sir Hugh Lane, another significant benefactor, endowed the collection with outstanding gifts both before and after his death in 1915, including works by Claude and Hogarth. He also left part of his residual estate to the Gallery for the purchase of pictures. The Lane Fund, in operation since 1918, continues to contribute to the acquisition of artworks for the collection.

In 1950 the Irish writer George Bernard Shaw left one-third of his posthumous royalties to the Gallery. To date, 85 European and Irish works have been added to the collection through the Shaw Fund, by such diverse artists as Gérard, Pissarro, Signac, Nolde, Van Dongen, O'Conor and Yeats.

The collection was further enriched in 1950 when Sir Alfred Chester Beatty, an Irish-American mining mogul, presented 93 paintings to the nation, by artists such as Breton, Couture, Meissonier and Gérôme. In 1987 Sir Alfred and Lady Beit, long-standing patrons of the Gallery, gifted 17 exceptional works to the collection by Spanish, Dutch and British masters including Velázquez, Murillo, Goya, Metsu, Vermeer, Van Ruisdael, Raeburn and Gainsborough. That same year the Gallery received 14 twentieth-century works from the estate of Máire MacNeill Sweeney, which included excellent examples by Picasso and Gris.

The long-lost masterpiece *The Taking of Christ* by Caravaggio, discovered in a Jesuit house on Leeson Street in Dublin and placed in the Gallery on indefinite loan by the Jesuits, is arguably the most important work in the collection. In 1993 it was unveiled by Sir Denis Mahon, the renowned scholar and collector of seventeenth-century Italian art, who himself gifted eight Baroque pictures to the collection, including works by Guercino, Guido Reni and Domenichino. Sir Denis also donated his extensive personal archive and library to the Gallery in 2010. The Yeats Archive, presented to the Gallery by Anne Yeats in 1996, contains a wealth of archival material relating to Jack B. Yeats and his extended family. This archive complements the popular paintings by the artist in the collection.

The Gallery's most prominent holdings relate to the Irish collection. Among the numerous much-loved Irish works are *The Marriage of Strongbow and Aoife* by Maclise and *The Meeting on the Turret Stairs* by Burton. Other celebrated Irish artists include Hone, Barry, Hamilton, Osborne, O'Conor, Orpen, Leech and Henry. The Prints and Drawings collection comprises some 12,000 works, a highlight of which is the bequest of 31 Turner watercolours by Henry Vaughan in 1900.

Since 1998, generously supported by Irish Life & Permanent, the National Portrait Collection, housed at the Gallery, has been enhanced by a series of commissioned portraits of prominent figures from contemporary Irish life. The annual Hennessy Portrait Prize, launched in 2014, has further contributed to the growth of this significant collection. In 2016 the Gallery took back the historic Dargan and Milltown wings after a lengthy period of refurbishment. The Gallery's ambition is to press ahead with the final phase of the Master Development Plan. This final phase will conclude a decade-long process of modernisation and essential improvement to provide a Gallery with world-class facilities for the enjoyment of future generations.

1300–1500

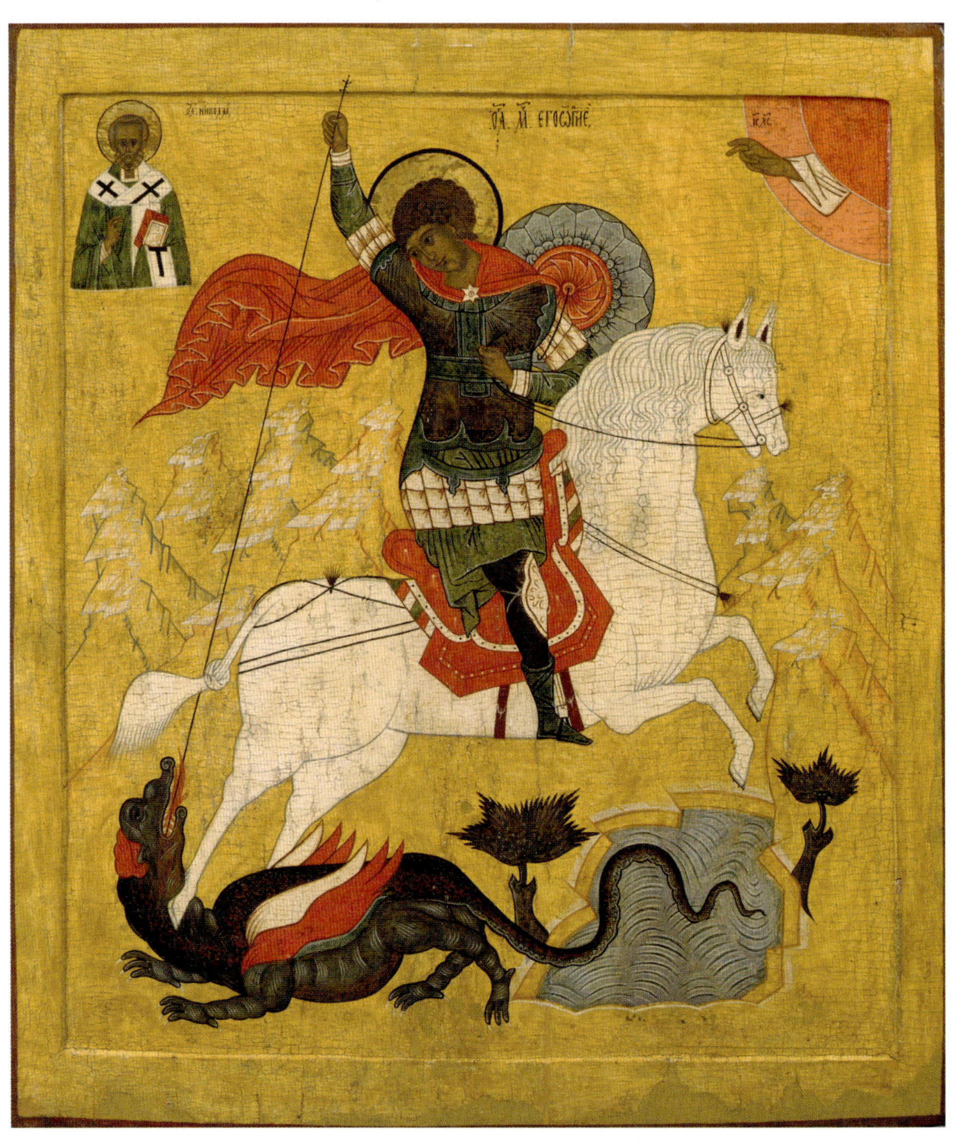

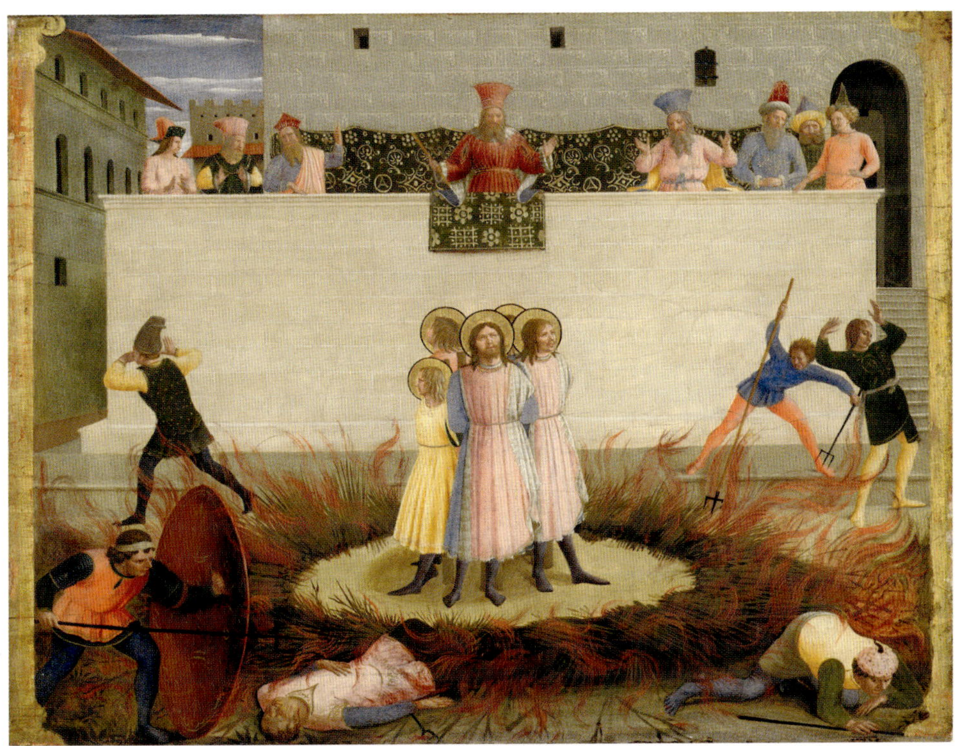

◄ **Unknown artist**

Novgorod, Russia, first half 15th century

St George and the Dragon, c.1400–1450

Tempera on wood panel, 73.5 x 63 cm
Purchased, 1968
NGI.1857

St George, a saint worshipped across the western and eastern worlds, was thought to have been a Roman soldier from the time of Diocletian. The most famous story about him is his rescue of a princess from a dragon, shown here as a fearsome beast pinned down by the saint's lance. St George is dressed in armour, and the pose he strikes with his circular shield is one long associated with depictions of eastern rulers. At the top right corner, the blessing hand of God appears, while on the left a bust of St Nicholas is depicted. Novgorod was at this time the principal Russian city and had access to the bright red cinnabar mineral that is used extensively on the panel.

▲ **Fra Angelico**

Florence c.1400–1455 Rome

Sts Cosmas and Damian and their Brothers Surviving the Stake, c.1439–1442

Tempera and gold leaf on wood panel, 37.8 x 46.4 cm
Purchased, 1886
NGI.242

This panel was part of the *predella*, or lower register, of Fra Angelico's most important altarpiece, created for the Dominican convent of San Marco in Florence. It was commissioned by Cosimo de' Medici. In third-century Asia Minor the Christian brothers Cosmas and Damian were subjected to persecution, initiated under the Roman Emperor Diocletian. When they refused to worship pagan gods, Lycias, the Roman consul, tortured them and attempted to kill them but they miraculously survived. This episode depicts the failed attempt to burn the brothers. Lycias and his dignitaries watch in dismay as the flames bounce away from the brothers and burn their persecutors.

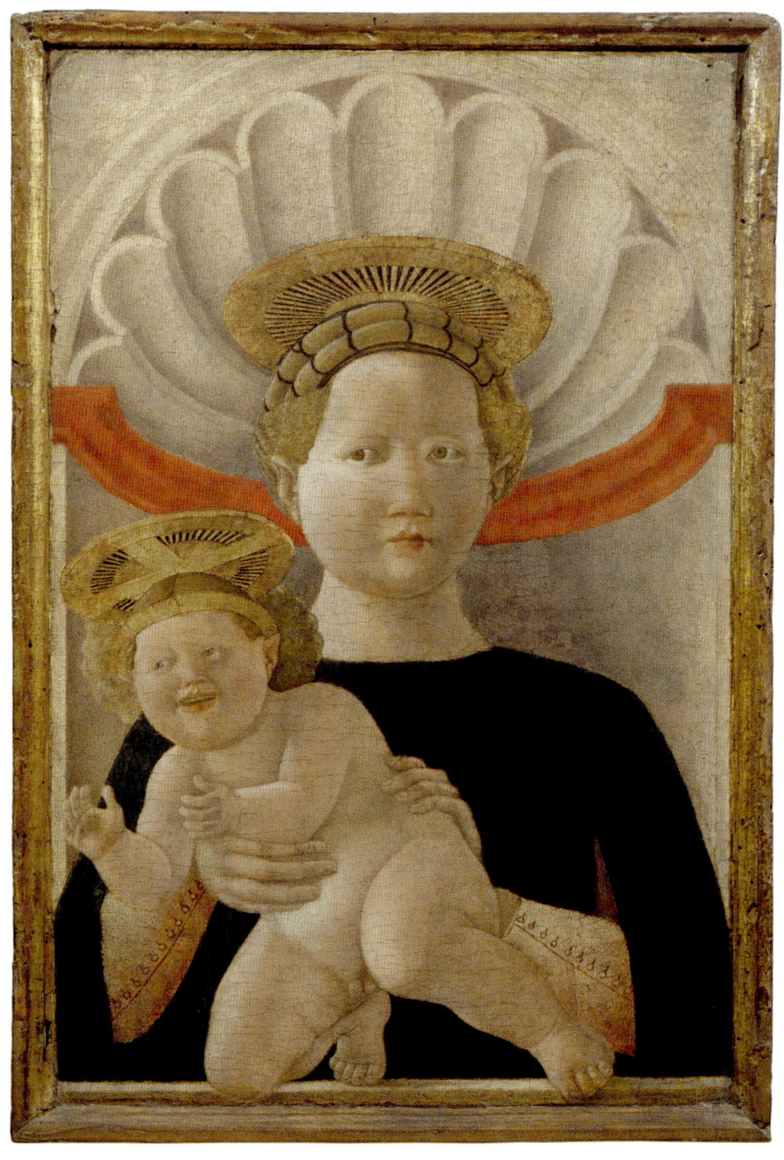

Paolo Uccello

Florence, c.1397–1475

The Virgin and Child, c.1435–1440

Tempera and gold leaf on wood panel, 58 x 37 cm
Purchased, 1909
NGI.603

A young Madonna, attired in a dark robe, emerges from the shadows of a shell-shaped niche. She holds a lively Christ Child, who appears ready to spring out of the picture space towards the spectator; his knee and toes rest on the edge of a false, painted frame. Both figures' haloes, painted in gold leaf, provide the illusion of three-dimensional ellipses. This panel illustrates Uccello's experimentation with geometry, perspective, space and light. In Florence, Uccello explored the system of linear perspective explained by the architect Leon Battista Alberti in his book *Della Pittura* (1435).

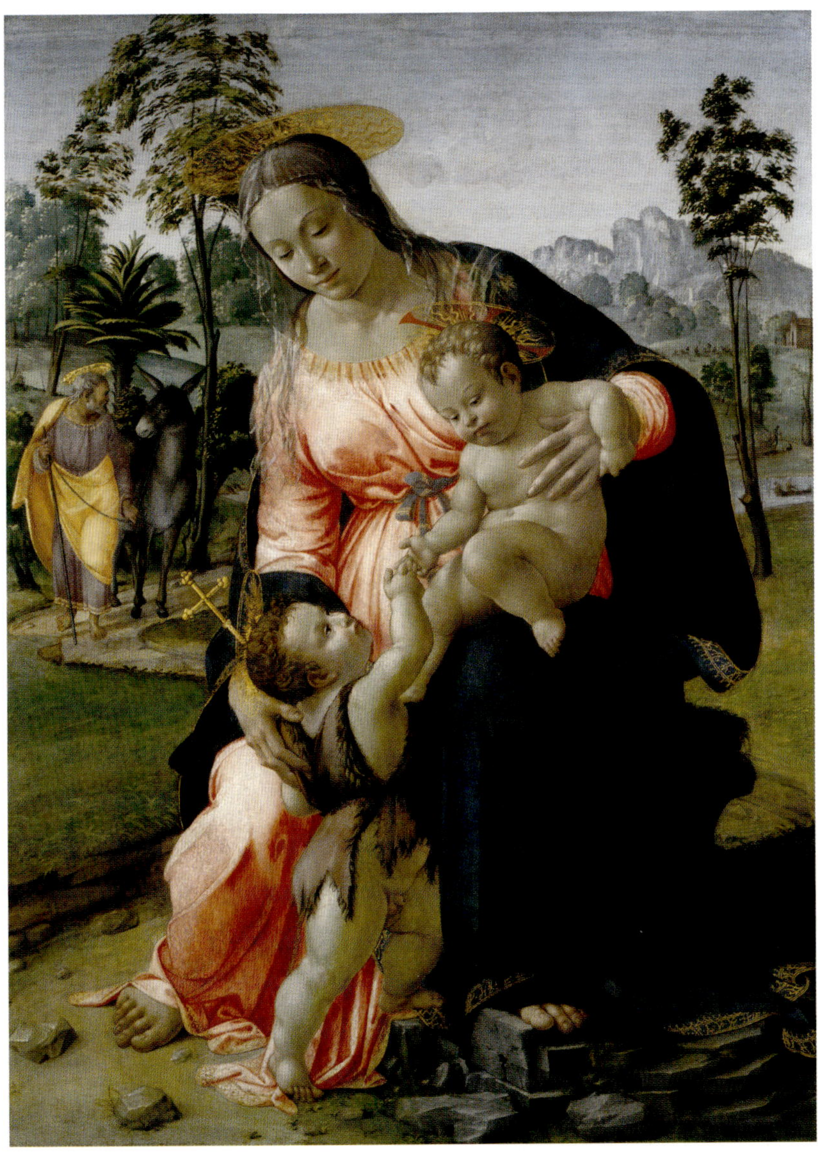

Francesco Granacci

Villamagna 1469–1543 Florence

Rest on the Flight into Egypt with the Infant St John the Baptist, c.1494

Tempera and oil on wood panel, 100 x 71 cm
Purchased, 1866
NGI.98

The scene is of the flight of the Holy Family into Egypt after Christ's birth, to escape King Herod. Appearing in St Matthew's Gospel, the story was considerably embellished in later texts. Jesus's young cousin, St John the Baptist, is shown here gently touching hands with Him. Behind is St Joseph, with the donkey that carried the Virgin and Christ. The landscape is more like Tuscany than the Holy Land. Granacci's friendship in Florence with Michelangelo is revealed by the sculptural quality of the main figure group.

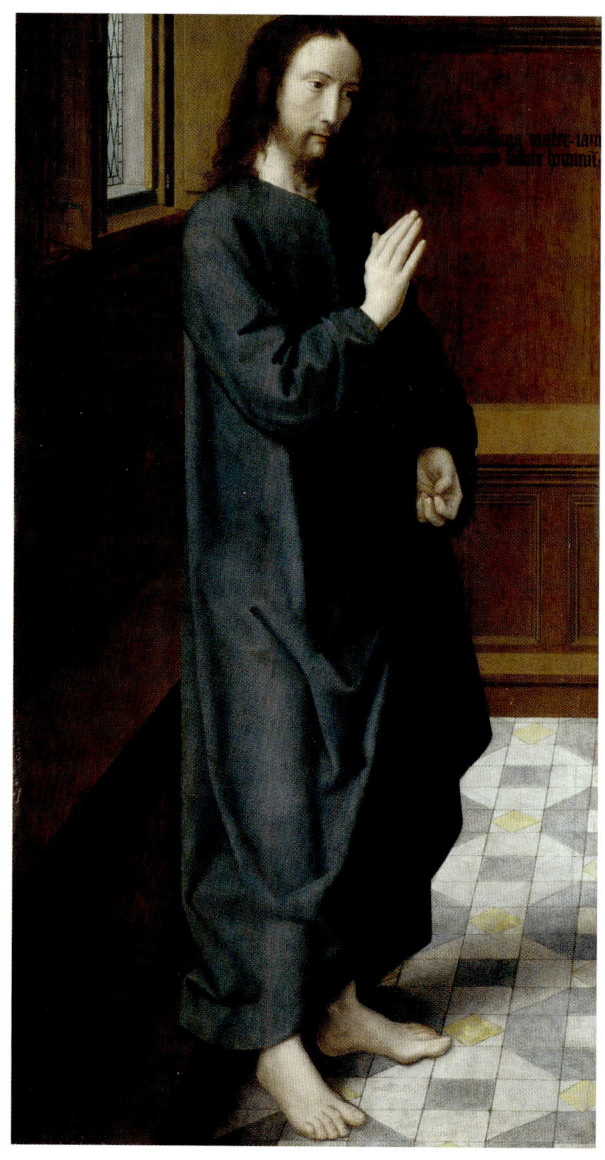

Gerard David

Oudewater c.1460–1523 Bruges

Christ Bidding Farewell to the Virgin, c.1498–c.1515

Oil on oak panel, 119.6 x 61.4 cm
Purchased, 1869
NGI.13

Born and trained in the northern Netherlands but flourishing as a master in Bruges, Gerard David was the last of the so-called 'Flemish Primitives'. This term is used to describe a group of fifteenth-century artists who introduced significant innovations to the technique of oil painting, allowing them to paint works with an unprecedented realistic effect. David was highly skilled in emulating the art of his predecessors, including Jan van Eyck, Hugo van der Goes and Hans Memling. The panel was probably originally part of a diptych. The other wing would have depicted the Virgin, to whom Christ is bidding farewell.

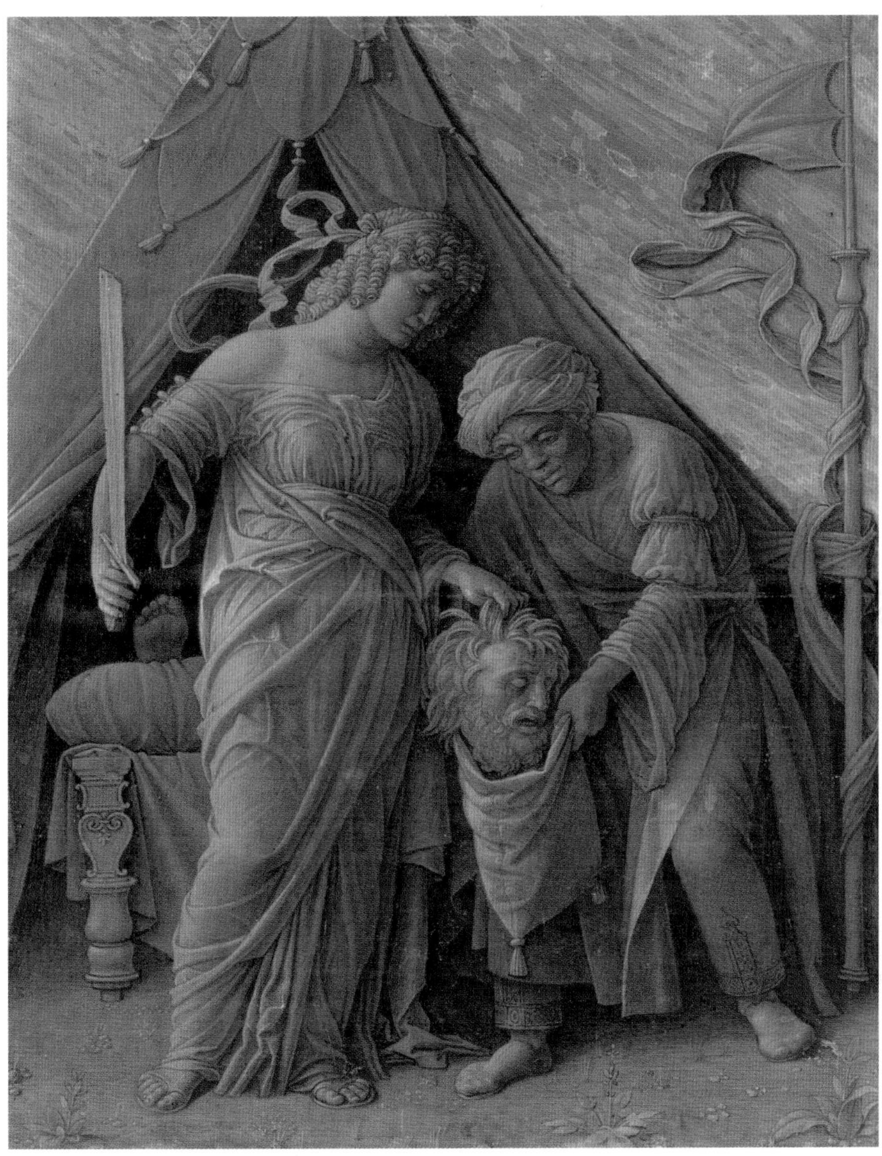

Andrea Mantegna

Padua c.1431–1506 Mantua

Judith with the Head of Holofernes, c.1495–1500

Tempera on linen, 48.1 x 36.7 cm
Purchased, 1896
NGI.442

The Old Testament Apocrypha tells the story of the Assyrians' siege of the Jewish city of Bethulia. Judith, a rich and pious widow, volunteers to kill the general of the enemy army, Holofernes. Gaining his confidence by seducing him, Judith waits until he falls asleep; she then severs his head with a sword and, with the help of her maidservant, conceals it in a sack. On discovering the headless corpse of their leader, the Assyrians flee. This painting illustrates Mantegna's fascination with antique sculpture: he has reduced his palette to shades of green, grey, orange and red, in imitation of various types of marble.

1500–1600

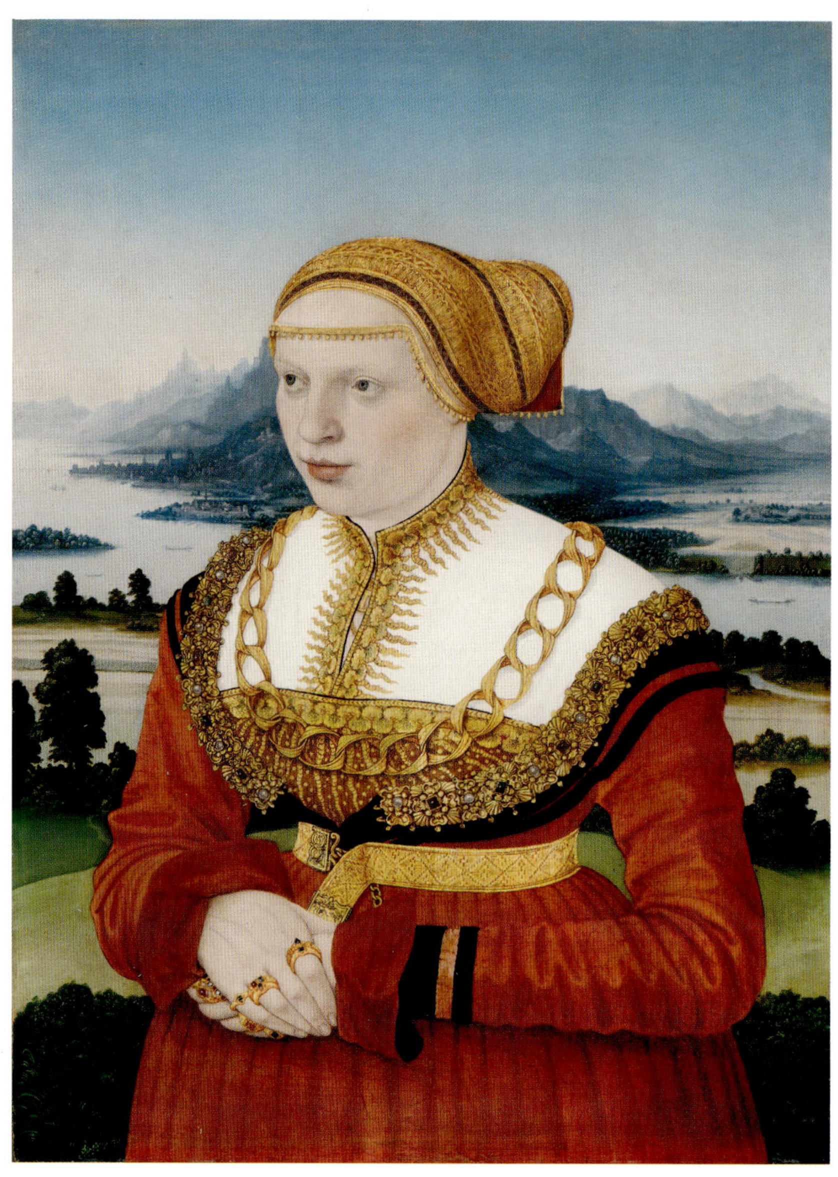

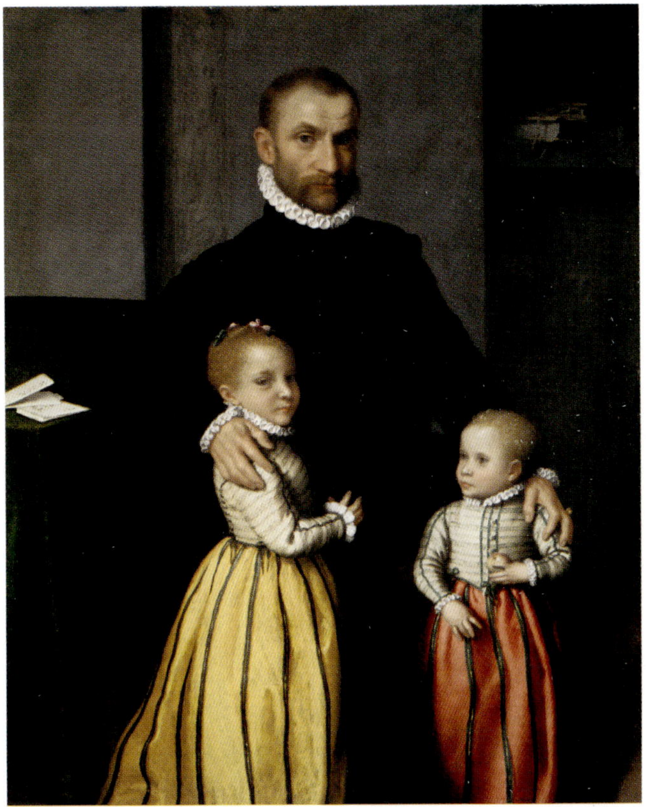

◀ **Conrad Faber von Creuznach**

Kreuznach c.1500–c.1553 Frankfurt am Main

Portrait of Katherina Knoblauch (1513–1542), 1532

Oil on limewood panel, 50.5 x 35.9 cm
Purchased, 1866
NGI.21

Katherina Knoblauch was a member of the ruling House of Limpurg in Frankfurt. Knoblauch means 'garlic', which explains the three garlic cloves in the family coat of arms on the reverse of this painting. In 1529 Katherina married Friedrich Rohrbach, and three years later Conrad Faber executed pendant portraits of the couple set against a panoramic landscape. Such fantastic views are common to most of Faber's portraits of the aristocracy in Frankfurt. The gold tooling in Katherina's head-dress and belt, the embroidery trimming her gown and her fine jewellery reflect her social status.

▲ **Giovanni Battista Moroni**

Albino c.1521/24–1579/80 Bergamo

Portrait of a Gentleman and his two Children, c.1572–1575

Oil on canvas, 125.3 x 98 cm
Purchased, 1866
NGI.105

A father, elegantly dressed in a black doublet with a narrow white ruff, protectively embraces his magnificently clad children. His dark attire may indicate that the man is a widower, although by 1570 the influence of sombre Spanish dress for men had replaced the more flamboyant costume fashionable in Italy until the late 1550s. The identity of the sitters is unknown but the setting is the artist's native Albino, a small town near Bergamo, indicated by the inscription on a letter on the table to the left. During the Renaissance, Moroni became one of the greatest portrait painters in northern Italy.

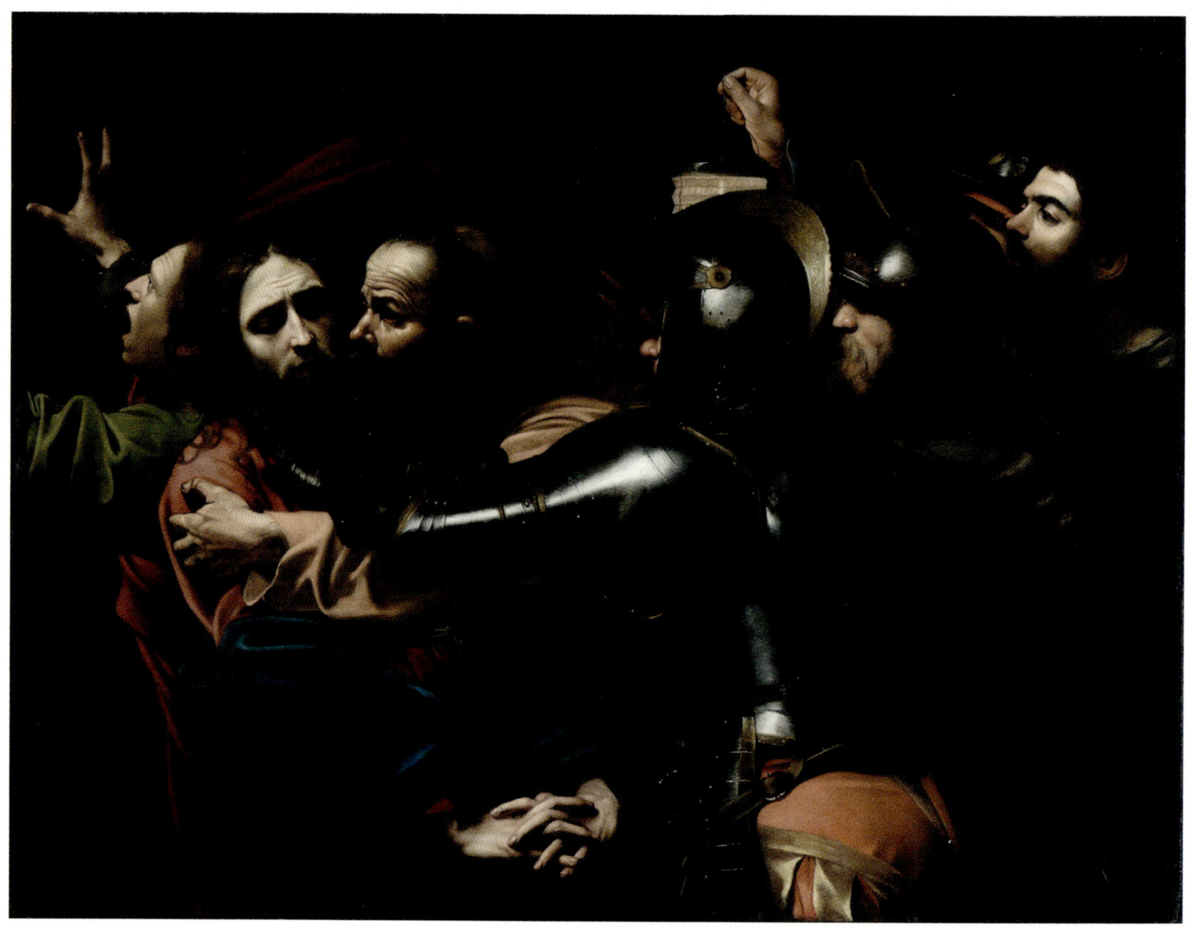

Caravaggio (Michelangelo Merisi da)
Caravaggio 1571–1610 Porto Ercole
The Taking of Christ, 1602

Oil on canvas, 135.5 x 169.5 cm
On indefinite loan to the National Gallery of Ireland from the Jesuit Community, Leeson St, Dublin, who acknowledge the kind generosity of the late Dr Marie Lea-Wilson, 1992
L.14702

Caravaggio depicts the dramatic moment from the Passion when Christ is betrayed by Judas in the garden of Gethsemane. The scene reaches an emotional pitch as the armoured guards surround Jesus, who offers no resistance to his destiny. The disciple shown fleeing on the left is St John the Evangelist. The figure at the far right, holding a lantern, is believed to be a self-portrait of the artist, who created this masterpiece at the peak of his career, employing his trademark realism, crowded picture space and *chiaroscuro* (the dramatic contrast between light and dark areas). These pioneering artistic devices made Caravaggio the most famous painter of his generation.

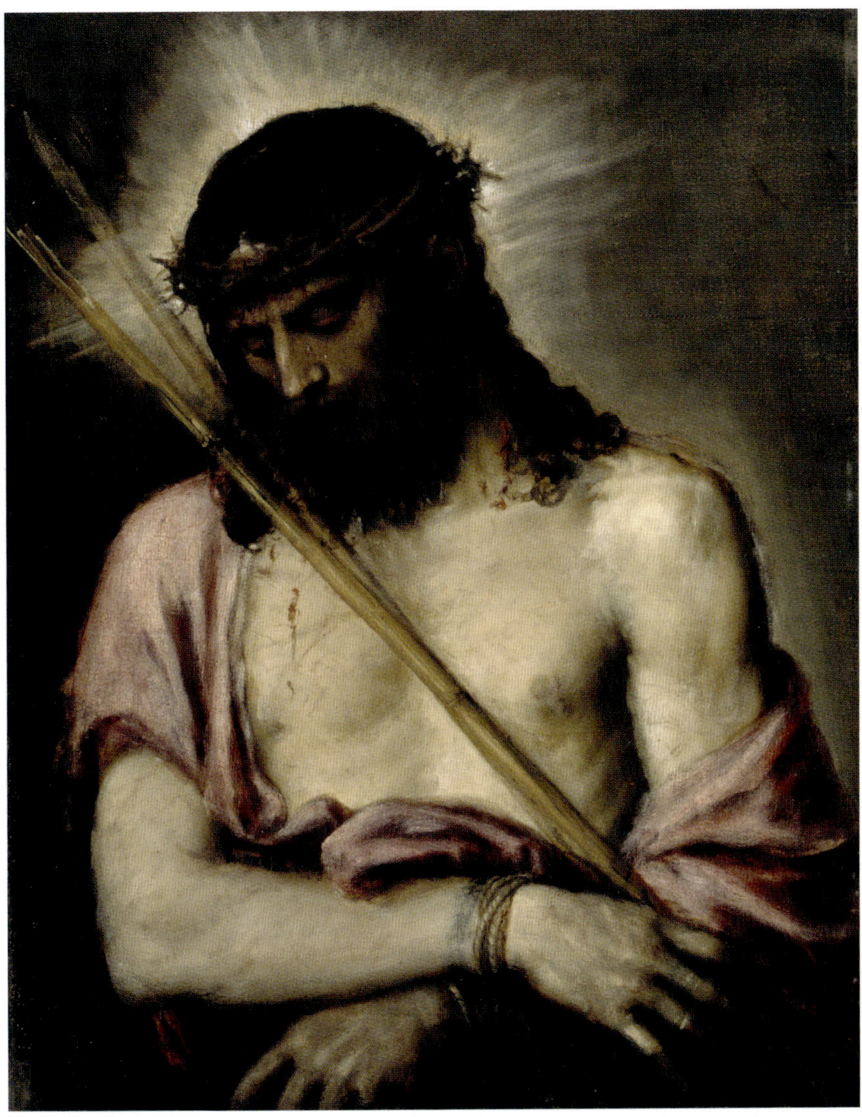

Titian (Tiziano Vecellio)

Pieve di Cadore c.1488–1576 Venice

Ecce Homo, 1558–1560

Oil on canvas, 73.4 x 56 cm
Purchased, 1885
NGI.75

Titian was the most talented Renaissance painter in Venice. His late works are imbued with a profound intensity and spirituality. During the Passion, having been flagellated and ridiculed with a crown of thorns, Jesus was presented by Pontius Pilate for the verdict of the people with the words *Ecce Homo* (Behold the Man). Images of the story were intended to arouse an emotive response in the viewer, and this is indeed a moving portrayal of physical suffering. It typifies Titian's late style, when he painted rapidly with loose brushstrokes and made adjustments, visible in the repositioning of the reed and the rope tied around Christ's wrists.

1600–1700

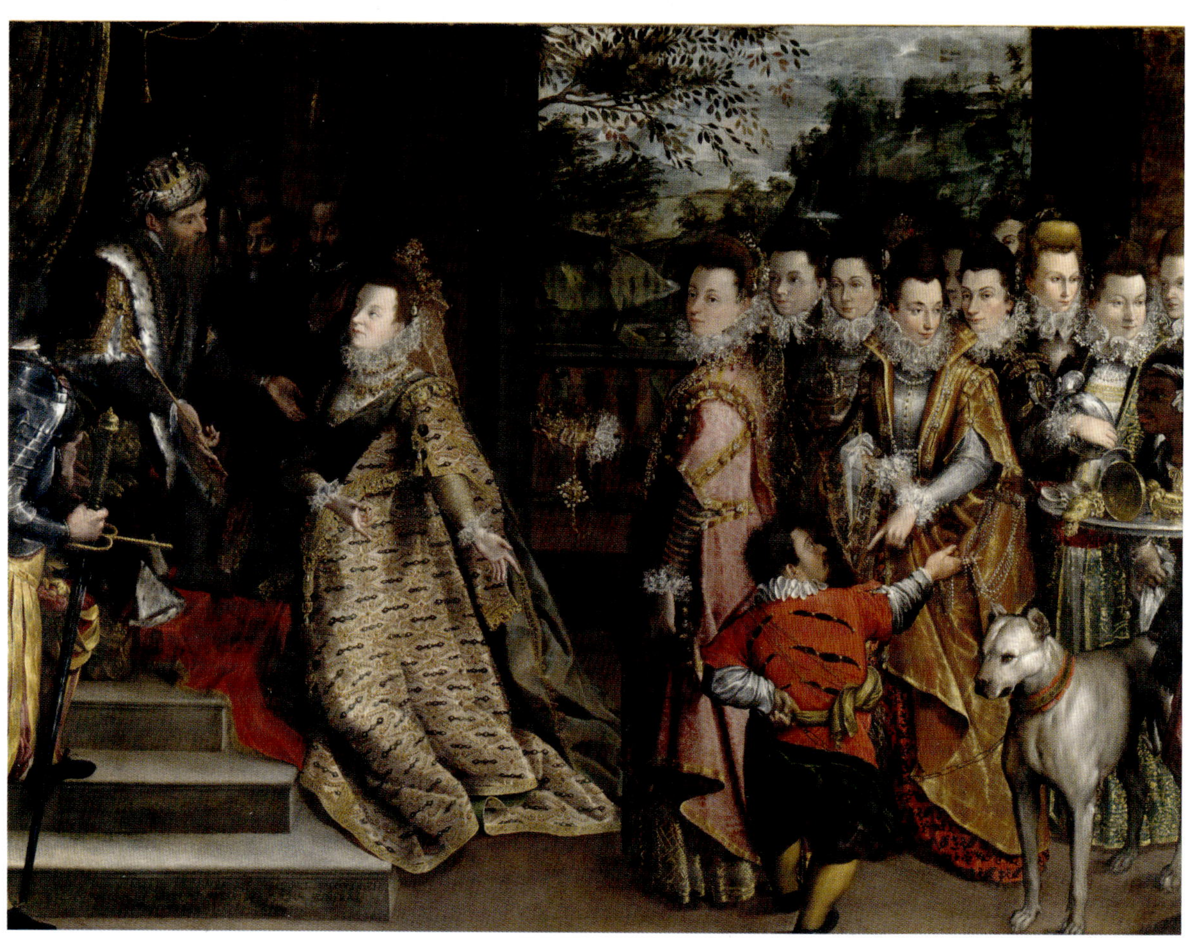

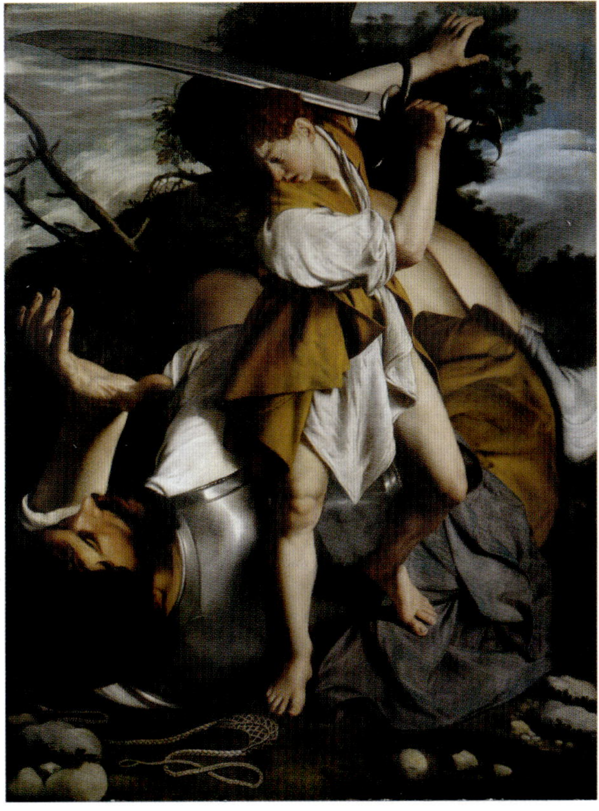

◄ **Lavinia Fontana**

Bologna 1552–1614 Rome

The Visit of the Queen of Sheba to King Solomon, c.1600

Oil on canvas, 256 x 325 cm
Purchased, 1872
NGI.76

Lavinia Fontana was a popular artist with the Italian nobility. In this, one of her most ambitious portraits, Vincenzo I Gonzaga and his wife Eleonora de' Medici are depicted in the guise of King Solomon and the Queen of Sheba. This Old Testament story was chosen because the Gonzaga family of Mantua claimed ancient connections with the Queen of Sheba. This work was apparently inspired by an actual event in 1600, when the Dukes of Mantua passed through Bologna on their way to attend the wedding in Florence of their relative Maria de' Medici and Henry IV of France.

▲ **Orazio Gentileschi**

Pisa 1563–1639 London

David and Goliath, c.1605–1607

Oil on canvas, 185.5 x 136 cm
Purchased, 1936 (Lane Fund)
NGI.980

The First Book of Samuel tells of Goliath, a great warrior of the Philistines, who challenges to fight any man from the Israelite army. David comes forward, armed with a sling and five stones. With the first stone he knocks Goliath down and then decapitates him with the giant's sword. In this work Gentileschi dramatically captures the moment before the beheading. The influence of Caravaggio's realism and his use of strong contrasts of light and shade is clearly evident. Goliath's hand, which seems about to burst out of the picture towards the viewer, enhances the scene's naturalism.

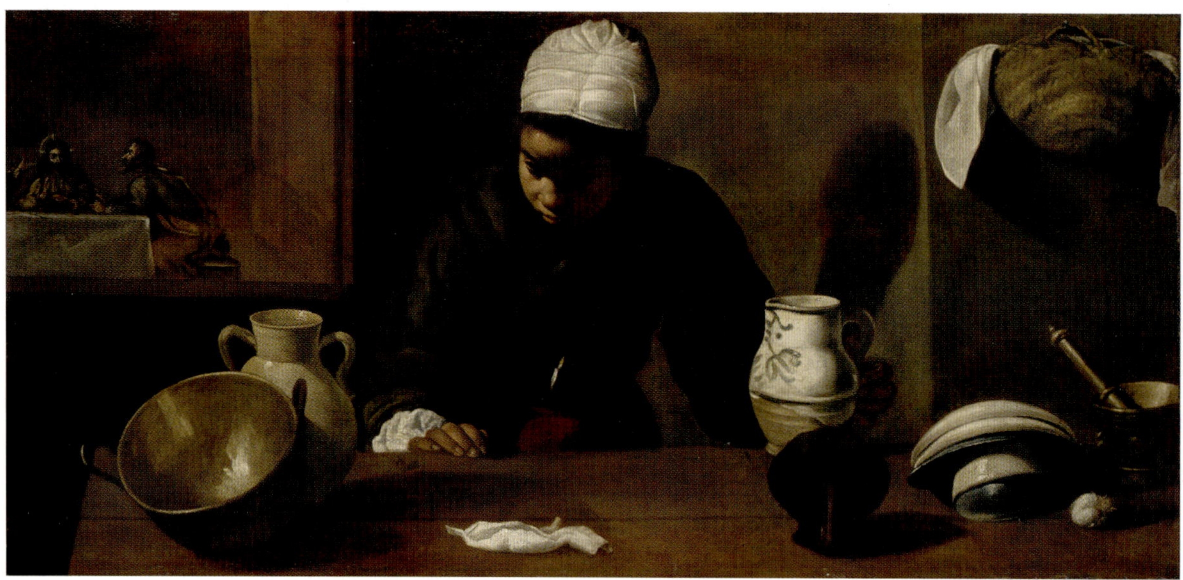

▲ **Diego Velázquez**
Seville 1599–1660 Madrid
Kitchen Maid with the Supper at Emmaus, c.1617–1618

Oil on canvas, 55 x 118 cm
Presented, Sir Alfred and Lady Beit, 1987
(Beit Collection)
NGI.4538

The scene of the Supper at Emmaus, where the resurrected Christ is revealed to two of his apostles, is visible through a hatch in the wall, while a kitchen maid appears to pause, as though aware of what is happening. The implication is that salvation is possible for her, as some Moors converted to Christianity in Spain. Velázquez painted this picture at the age of 18 or 19, when he was working in Seville under the influence of Caravaggio. It is considered to be his earliest known work and is one of several *bodegones*, which combined still life and genre in a kitchen or tavern setting. Some of these included a religious scene to increase their value.

▶ **Jan Breughel the Younger**
Antwerp, 1601–1678
Peter Paul Rubens
Siegen 1577–1640 Antwerp
Christ in the House of Martha and Mary, c.1628

Oil on oak panel, 64 x 61.9 cm
Bequeathed, Sir Henry Page Turner Barron, 1901
NGI.513

In the gospel of St Luke, the two sisters of Lazarus react differently when Christ visits their home. Mary of Bethany listens attentively to his words, while Martha busies herself with housework. Martha's concern with the active, material life is illustrated by her rolled-up sleeves and dishevelled apron, while Mary's interest in the spiritual life is indicated by her contemplative pose; the contrast between the two was a popular theme in seventeenth-century art. This picture is a collaboration between two artists: Jan Breughel the Younger painted the birds, animals, fruit and flowers in detail, while Rubens painted the drapery, poses and facial expressions more fluidly.

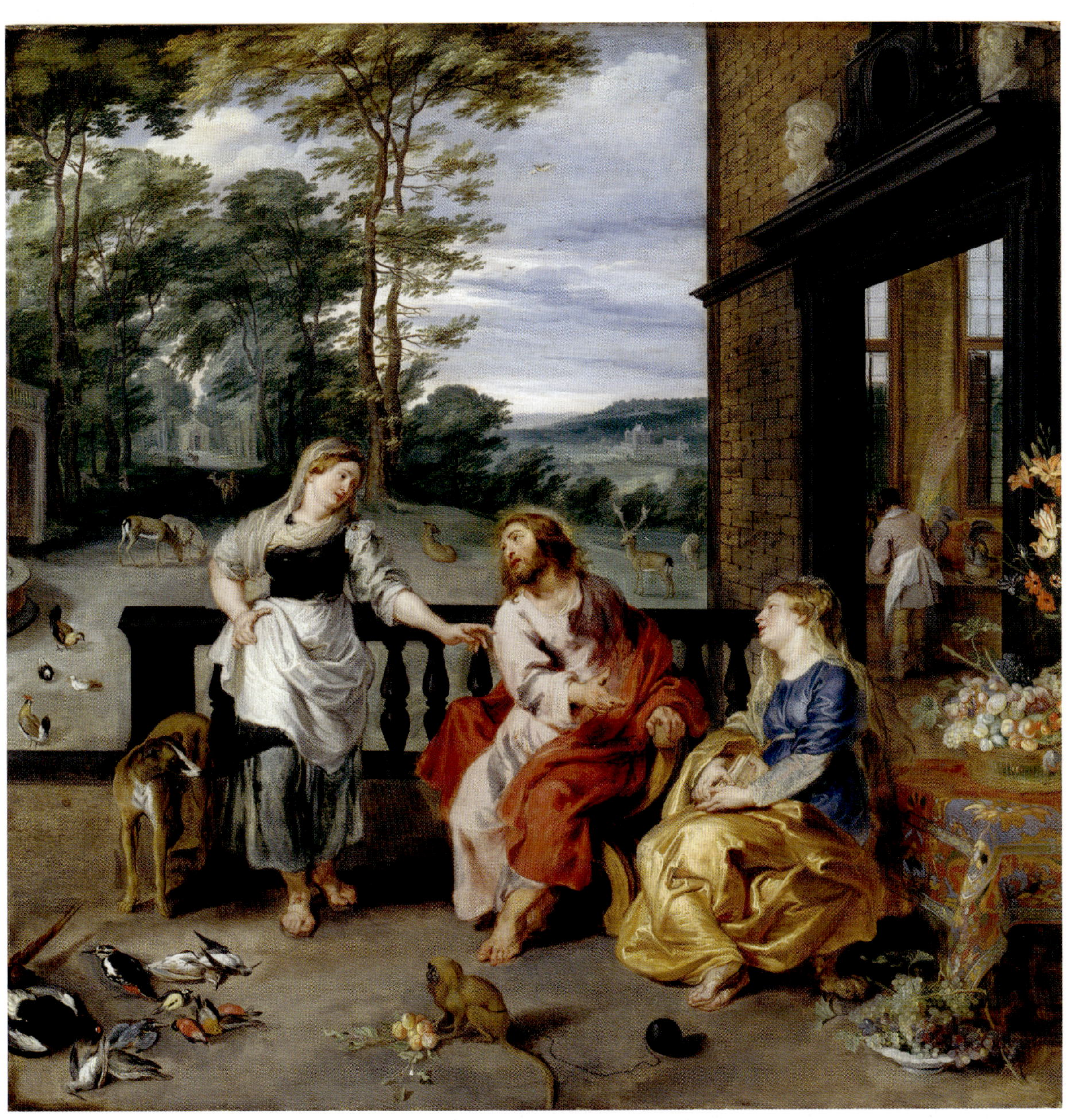

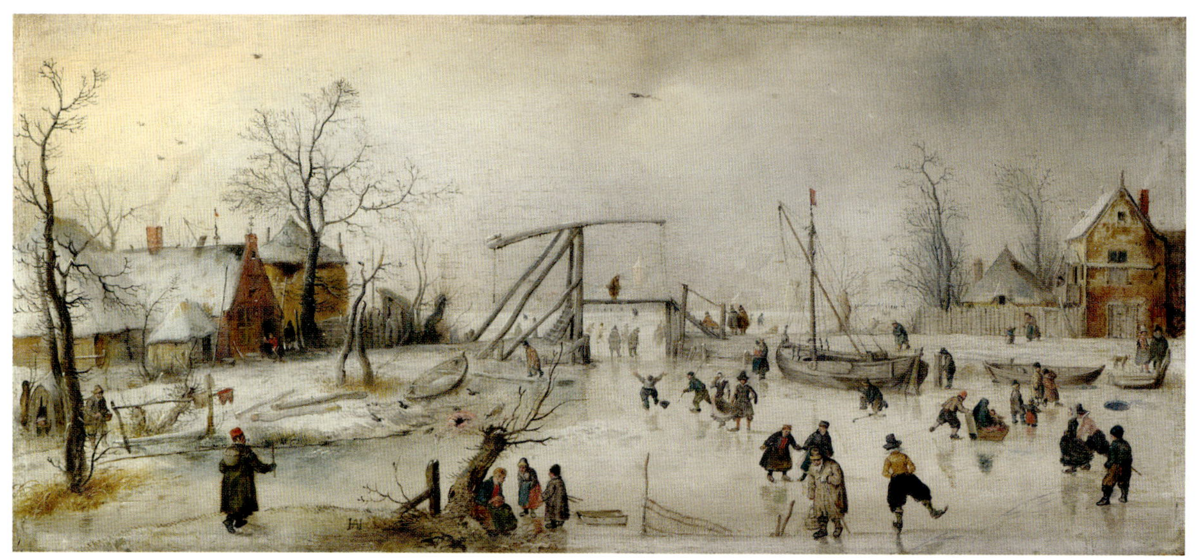

Hendrick Avercamp

Amsterdam 1585–1634 Kampen

Scene on the Ice, c.1620

Oil on wood panel, 20.5 x 43.8 cm
Presented, T. Humphry Ward, 1900
NGI.496

The depiction of the seasons in art was elevated to new heights by the Flemish painter Pieter Bruegel the Elder, who taught Avercamp's master, Pieter Isaacsz, and whose winter scenes Avercamp studied closely. Avercamp became the principal Dutch practitioner of the winter landscape. This frozen canal is populated by people who skate for pleasure or go about their daily activities. Some move with confidence while others skid on the ice. The artist's acute observation of everyday life is evident in details such as the hole cut in the ice for fishing, while his treatment of light suggests the frosty atmosphere and leaden sky of winter.

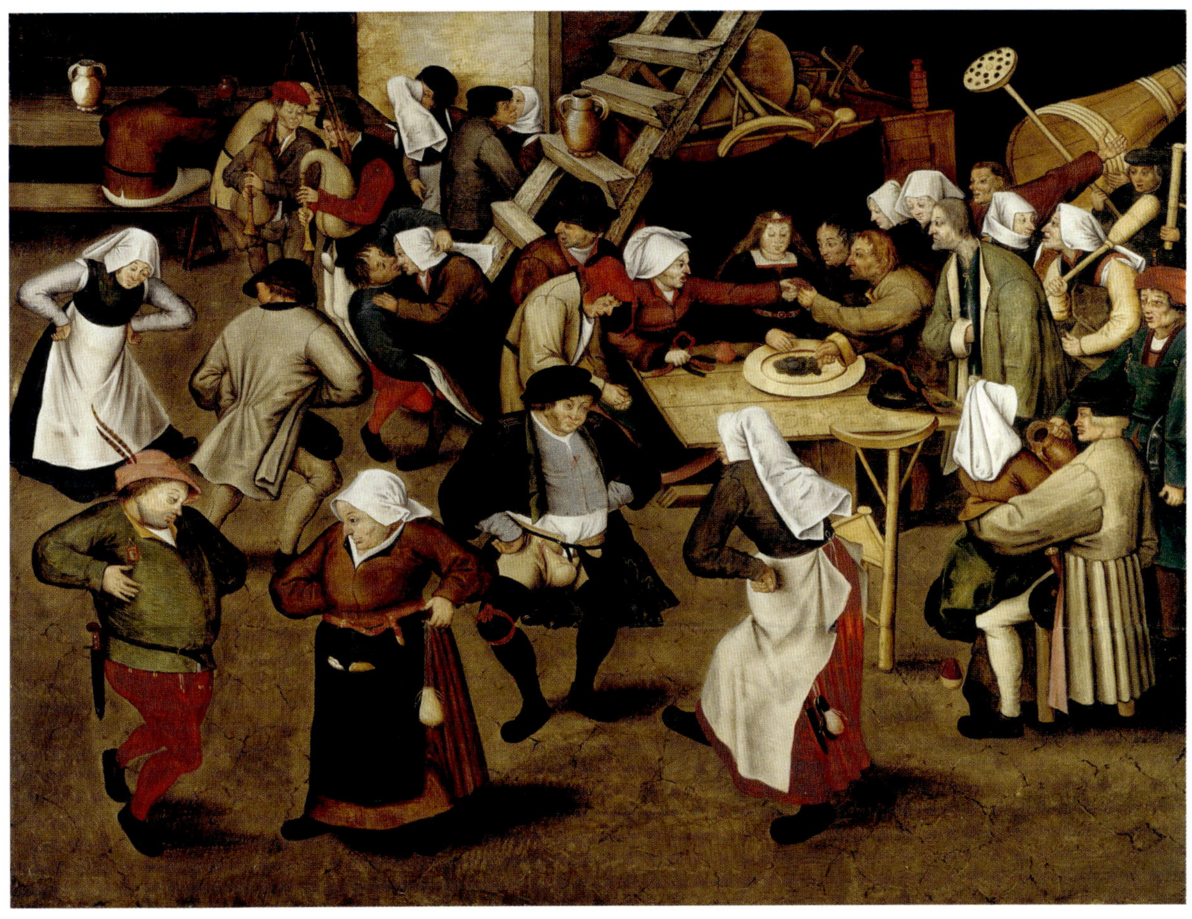

Pieter Brueghel the Younger
Brussels 1564–1638 Antwerp
Peasant Wedding, 1620

Oil on wood panel, 81.5 x 105.2 cm
Purchased, 1928
NGI.911

A bride looks down at her dowry plate as an old woman grabs a money pouch offered by a guest. In Brueghel's animated portrayal of a country wedding, the peasants' facial expressions and posturing are exaggerated to the point of caricature. They enjoy dance, music, alcohol and love-making, and their uninhibited behaviour may warn against over-indulgence, turning this burlesque into a satire with a moral message. The carvings on the table-top include a windmill, a heart pierced with arrows, a wine flask, an owl and two intertwined fish. While some of these may be symbolic, others may simply be score marks in the wood related to game-playing.

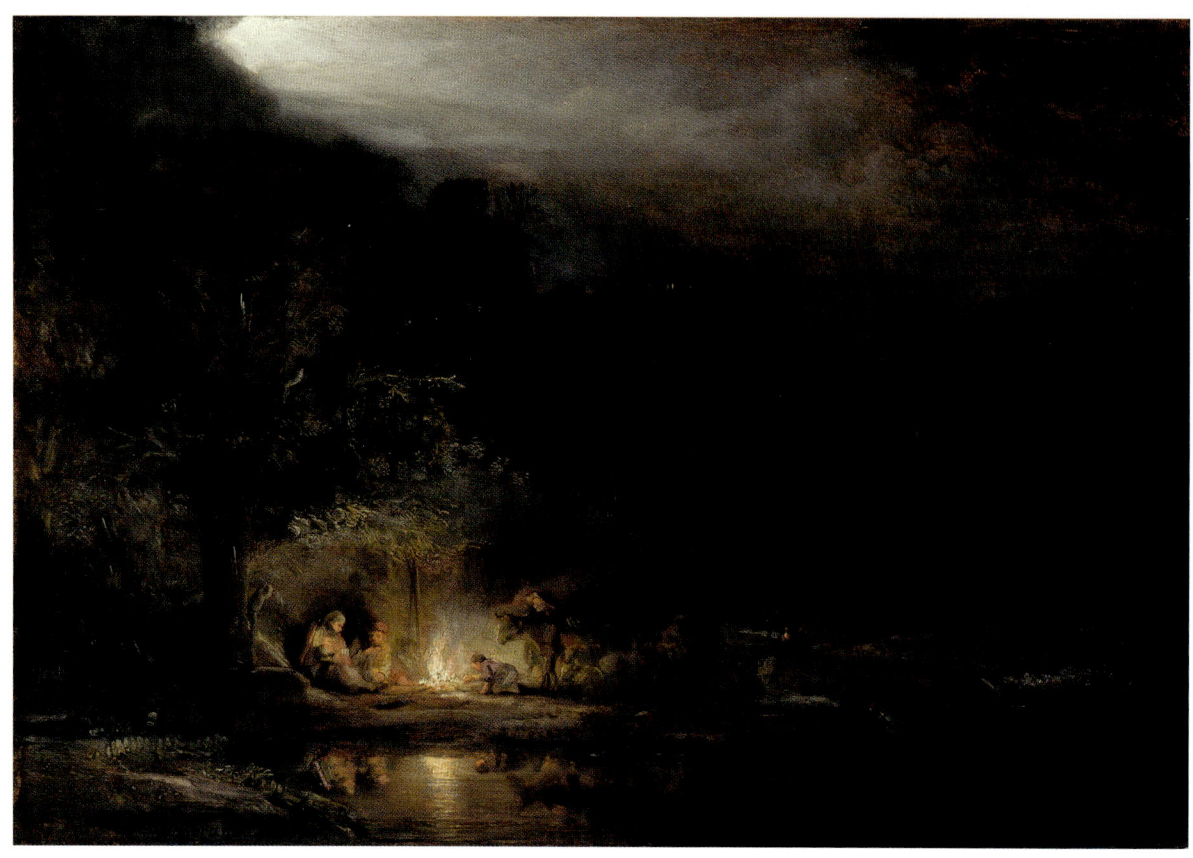

Rembrandt van Rijn

Leiden 1606–1669 Amsterdam

Landscape with the Rest on the Flight into Egypt, 1647

Oil on wood panel, 34 x 48 cm
Purchased, 1883
NGI.215

After the birth of Christ, the Holy Family fled Bethlehem to avoid the massacre of the newborn that had been ordered by King Herod. In this nocturnal scene the family settle by a fire, tended by a boy, while shepherds approach with their animals. The flames, rendered with thick pigment, are reflected in a pool, and a dense forest is silhouetted by moonlight. Clouds sweep across the sky, blocking out the moon itself, and a fortified castle looms in the distance. The diagonal composition was inspired by that of Adam Elsheimer's *Rest on the Flight into Egypt* (1609), engraved in 1613–14. Rembrandt must have known the engraving, if not the painting itself.

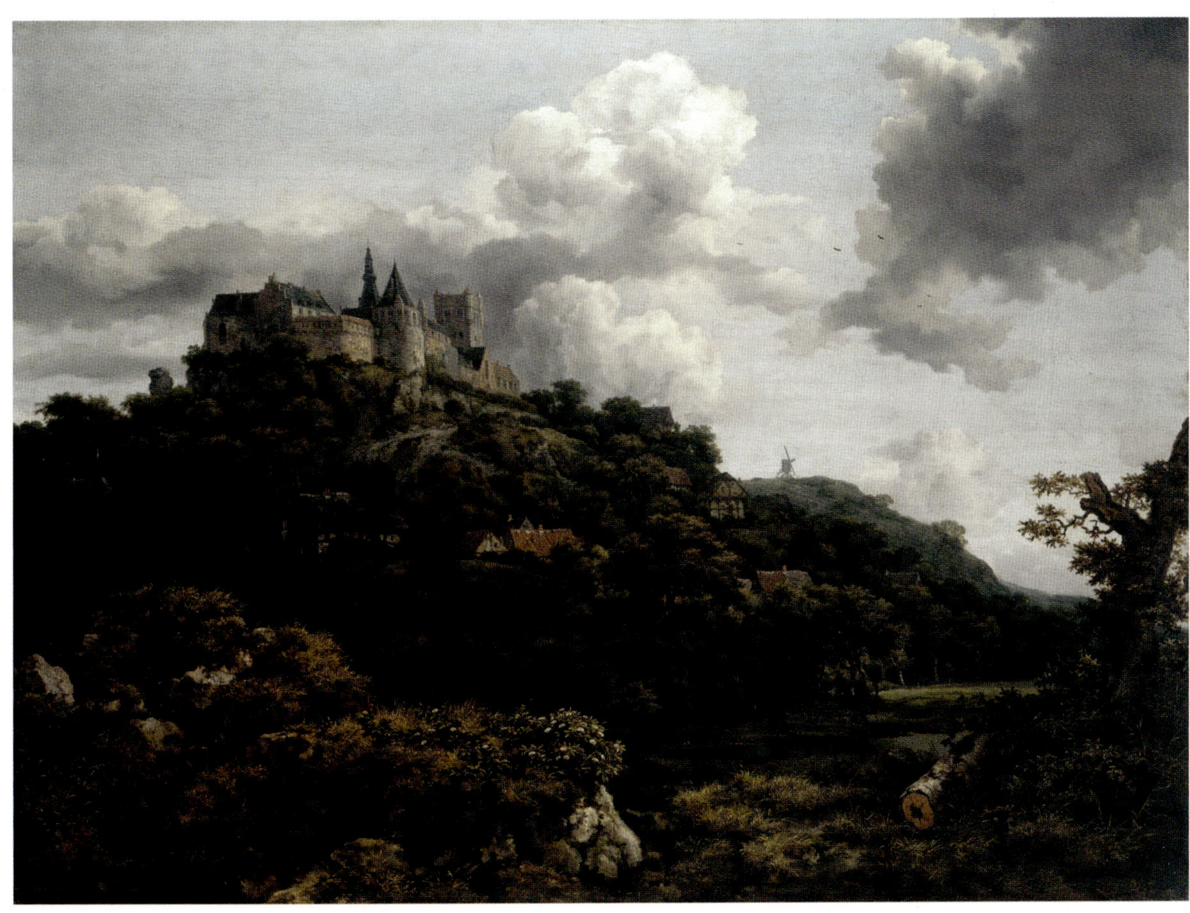

Jacob van Ruisdael

Haarlem 1628/29–1682 Amsterdam

The Castle of Bentheim, 1653

Oil on canvas, 110.5 x 144 cm
Presented, Sir Alfred and Lady Beit, 1987
(Beit Collection)
NGI.4531

Active in Haarlem and later in Amsterdam, Van Ruisdael is widely regarded as the finest Dutch landscape painter of the seventeenth century. He painted over 1,000 pictures, and this majestic landscape is acknowledged as a masterpiece. Van Ruisdael visited Bentheim, a small town in the German province of Westphalia near the border with Holland, in about 1650. He painted at least 14 views of the castle, exaggerating its appearance and location to emphasise the power of nature. Here the prospect of the medieval castle is romanticised and more elevated than it is in reality.

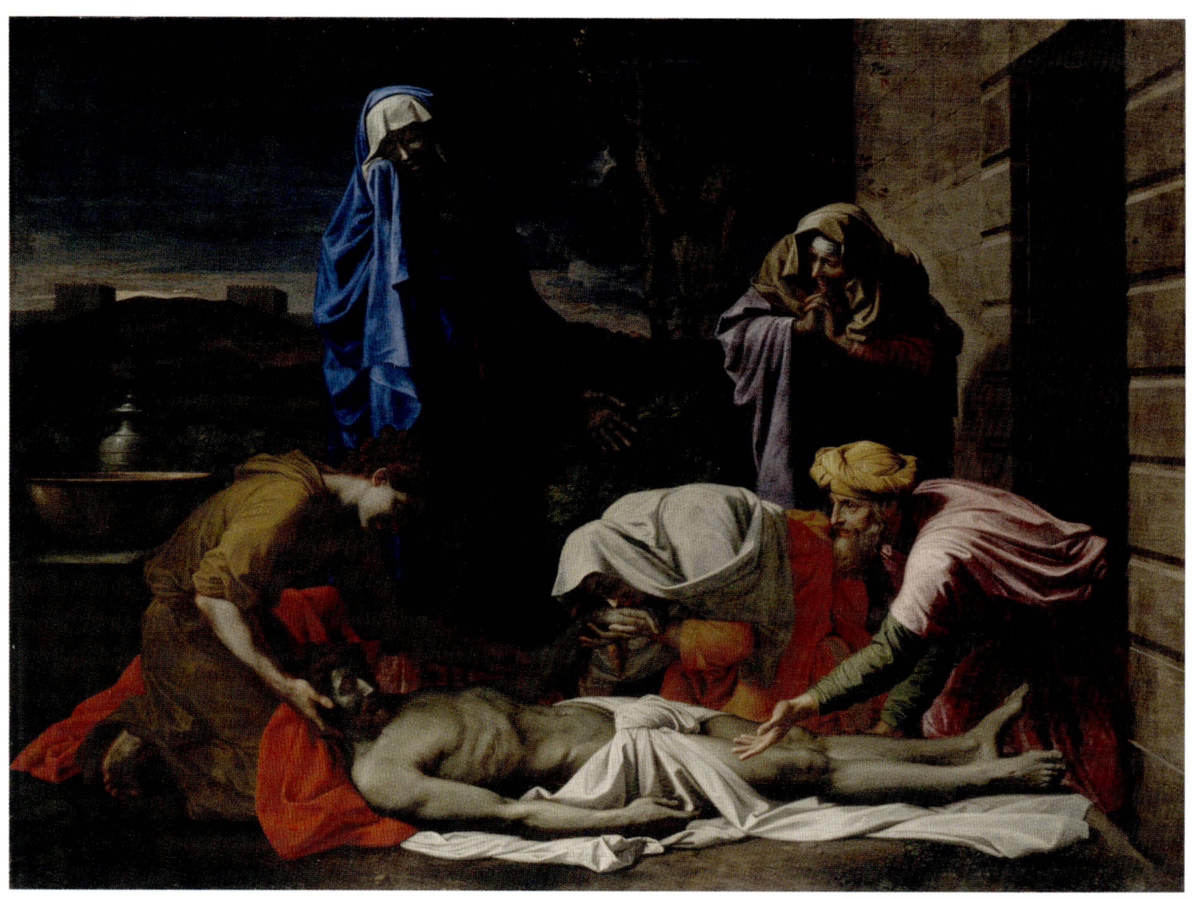

Nicolas Poussin

Les Andelys 1594–1665 Rome

The Lamentation over the Dead Christ, 1657

Oil on canvas, 94 x 130 cm
Purchased, 1882
NGI.214

Poussin was a French Neo-classical painter who spent most of his working life in Rome. This painting, veiled in darkness and solemn in mood, is one of his late works. It depicts the sombre moment before Christ's body is placed in the tomb. His mother and closest disciples join each other in mourning. The Virgin wipes away her tears with her cloak; its intense blue colour emphasises the depth of her grief. In the background, a tree bearing new shoots alludes to Christ's Resurrection.

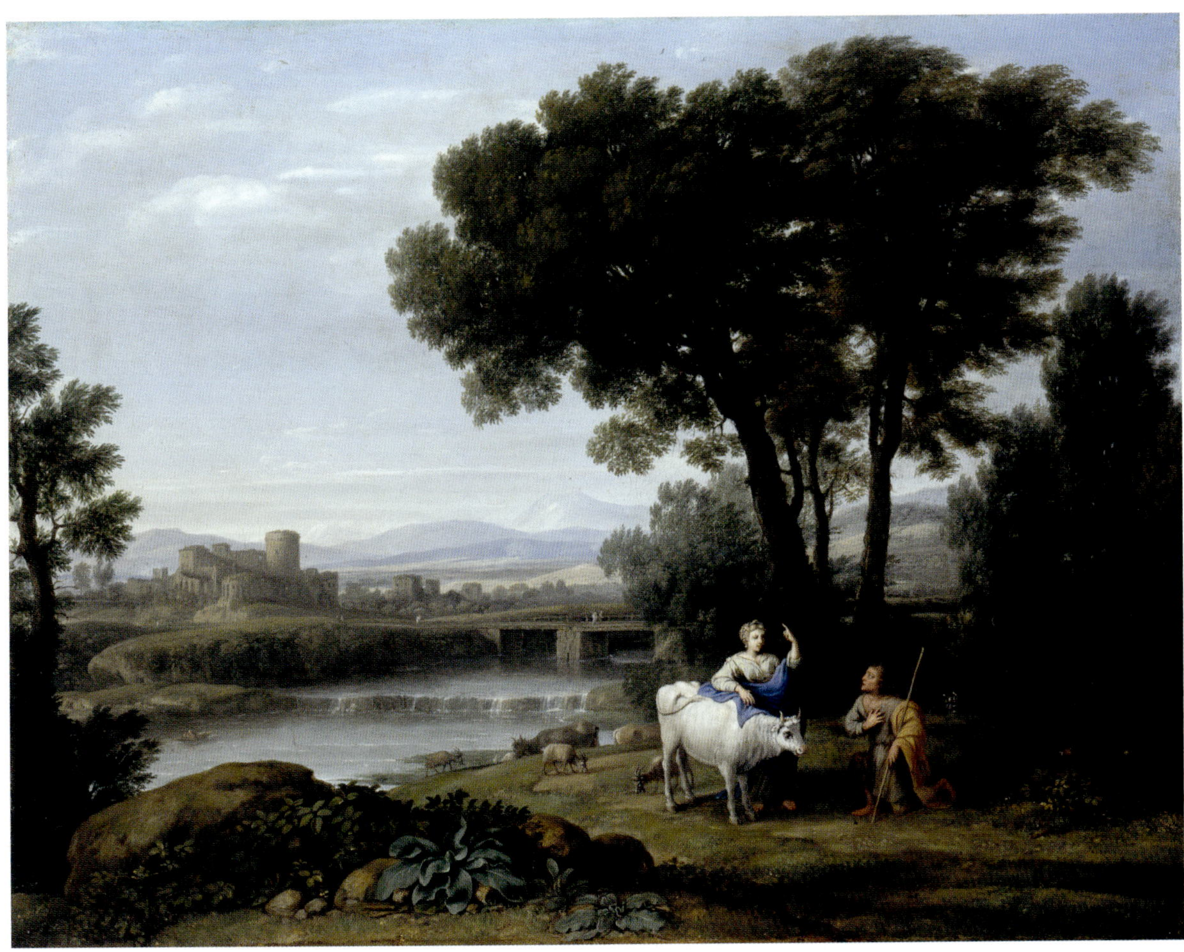

Claude Lorrain

Chamagne 1604–1682 Rome

Juno Confiding Io to the Care of Argus, 1660

Oil on canvas, 60 x 75 cm
Bequeathed, Sir Hugh Lane, 1918
NGI.763

In an episode from Ovid's *Metamorphoses* Jupiter seduces Io and transforms her into a white heifer to conceal her from his wife, Juno. Juno is not deceived and asks her husband for the cow as a gift, which she gives into the custody of Argus, the hundred-eyed giant. Claude depicts the moment when Juno entrusts the heifer to Argus, depicted here as a shepherd. He has imbued this idealised landscape with a nostalgic spirit of antiquity. Like the artist's other landscapes, it is not a record of an actual location but an evocation of a bygone era, inspired by the terrain of the Roman Campagna.

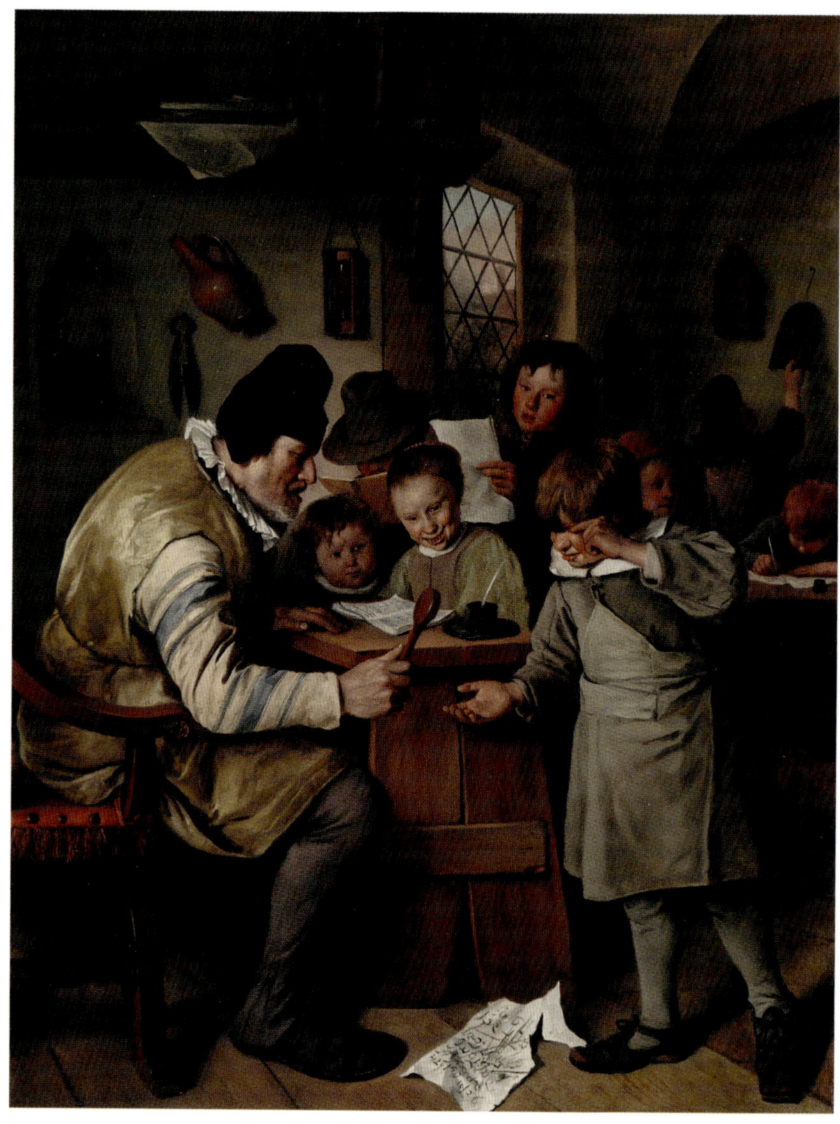

Jan Steen

Leiden, 1626–1679

The Village School, c.1665

Oil on canvas, 110.5 x 80.2 cm
Purchased, 1879
NGI.226

One of the key painters of the Dutch Golden Age, Steen is best known for his depictions of dissolute households, which often incorporated a moralising theme and frequently illustrated Dutch sayings. These cheerful and disorderly scenes seem to be a combination of narrative, instruction and entertainment. *The Village School* depicts a boy being punished by a teacher. Among the objects on the wall are boxes used by children for bringing their books to school. Steen also places bottles in a niche on the left of the painting. Many schoolteachers doubled up as landlords in seventeenth-century Holland, which lead authors, painters and printmakers to portray them as alcoholics.

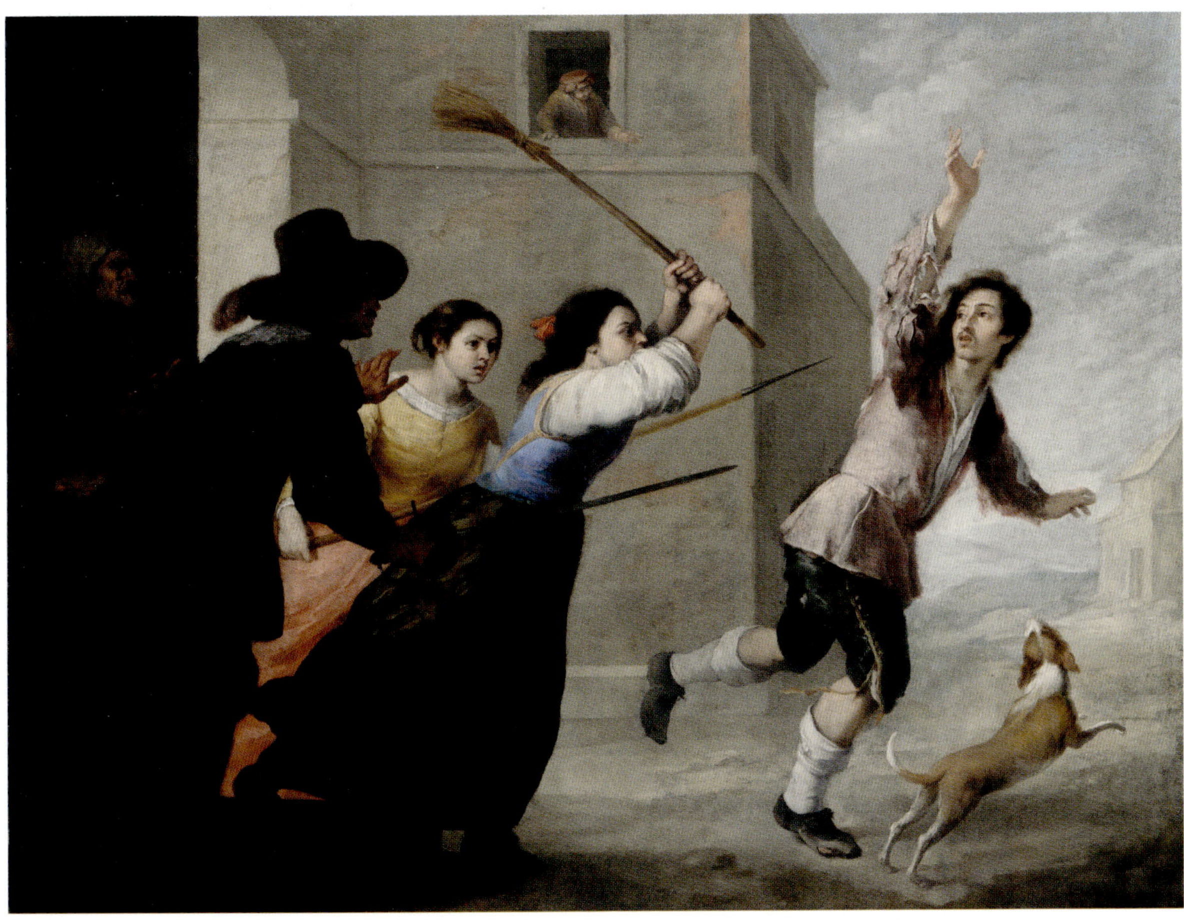

Bartolomé Esteban Murillo

Seville, 1617–1682

The Prodigal Son Driven Out, 1660s

Oil on canvas, 104.5 x 134.5 cm
Presented, Sir Alfred and Lady Beit, 1987
(Beit Collection)
NGI.4543

In the parable of the Prodigal Son from St Luke's Gospel, a young man squanders his inheritance on enjoying himself with harlots and must then face the consequences. Murillo imagines the dramatic moment where the man is expelled from his house, using the setting of seventeenth-century Seville, where he was the principal artist. This is one of six paintings in the Gallery's collection that tell the story. The movement of the figures is echoed by Murillo's swift painting technique and the artist uses a rich palette, unlike the black and red colours used in many, more sober, religious depictions.

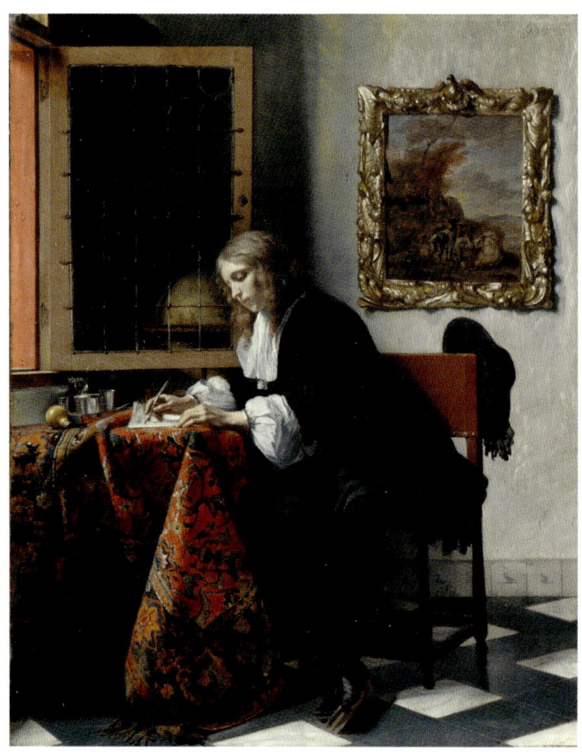

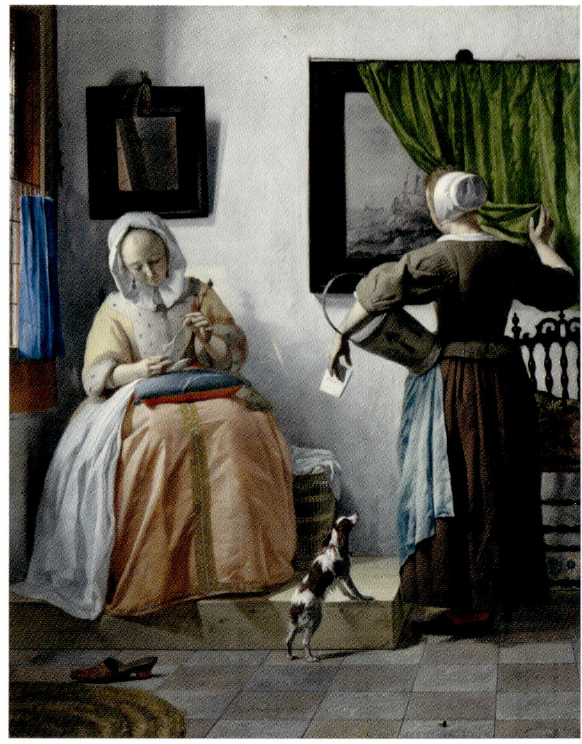

Gabriel Metsu

Leiden 1629–1667 Amsterdam

Man Writing a Letter, 1664–1666

Oil on wood panel, 52.5 x 40.5 cm
Presented, Sir Alfred and Lady Beit, 1987
(Beit Collection)
NGI.4536

Metsu was one of the most accomplished and versatile genre painters of his time. This painting and its counterpart, *Woman Reading a Letter* (NGI.4537), are Metsu's most famous works and belong to the finest Dutch genre paintings produced in the seventeenth century. Both pictures reveal the influence of Johannes Vermeer. The theme of letter-writing enjoyed great popularity among Dutch genre painters of the 1650s–60s. This painting depicts a gentleman writing a letter for the lady represented in its pendant. The man's fashionable black costume and the Persian carpet on the table suggest that he is well-to-do.

Gabriel Metsu

Leiden 1629–1667 Amsterdam

Woman Reading a Letter, 1664–1666

Oil on wood panel, 52.5 x 40.2 cm
Presented, Sir Alfred and Lady Beit, 1987
(Beit Collection)
NGI.4537

Engrossed in her suitor's letter, a lady holds the sheet at an angle, not simply because she needs more light to read it but also because she wants to hide the contents from her maid. Yet her servant already knows what the letter is about. She is seen to issue a warning to her mistress by pulling aside a curtain to reveal a painting of a ship sailing on choppy waters, a reference to the then common simile that love is like a rough sea. Metsu originally intended the lady's jacket to be red but changed it to yellow to allude to similar garments in Vermeer's paintings.

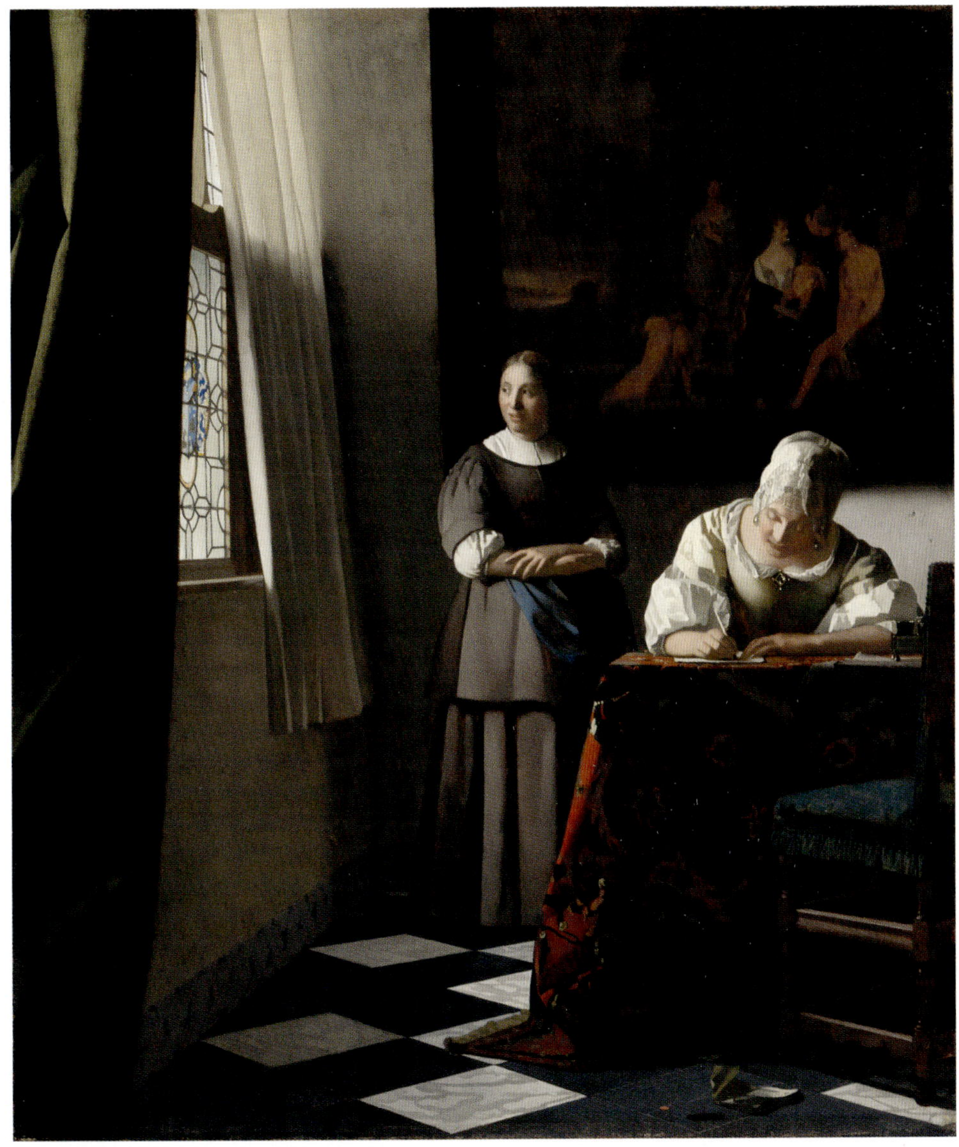

Johannes Vermeer

Delft, 1632–1675

Woman Writing a Letter, with her Maid, c.1670

Oil on canvas, 71.1 x 60.5 cm
Presented, Sir Alfred and Lady Beit, 1987
(Beit Collection)
NGI.4535

Vermeer's work displays an unprecedented level of artistic mastery in its illusion of reality. His figures are often quiet and inactive, which contributes to the solemn and mysterious atmosphere of his paintings. *Woman Writing a Letter* is one of the most ingenious compositions of the artist's late career. While a maidservant gazes out of a window, her mistress writes an epistle. In the foreground on the floor lie a red seal, a stick of sealing wax and an object which is either a crumpled letter or a letter-writing manual, a standard aid for personal correspondence at the time.

1700–1800

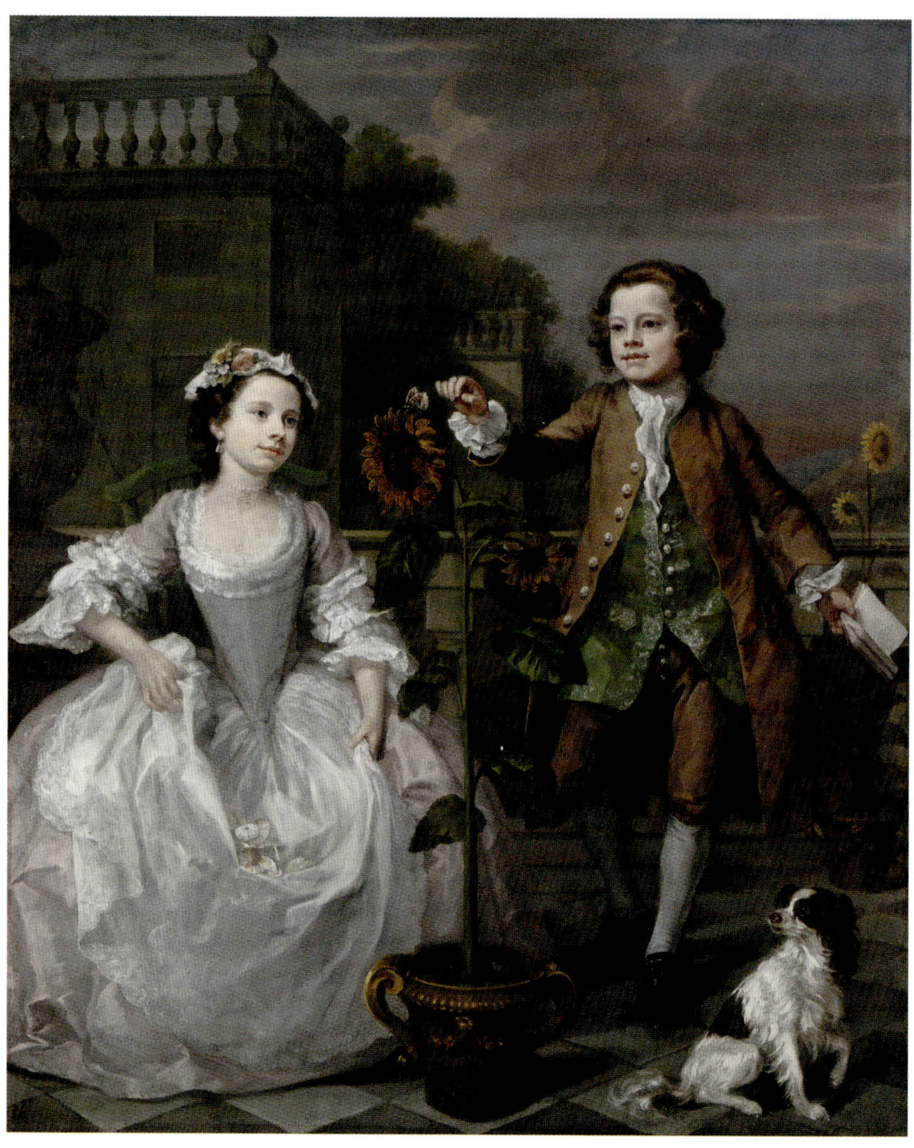

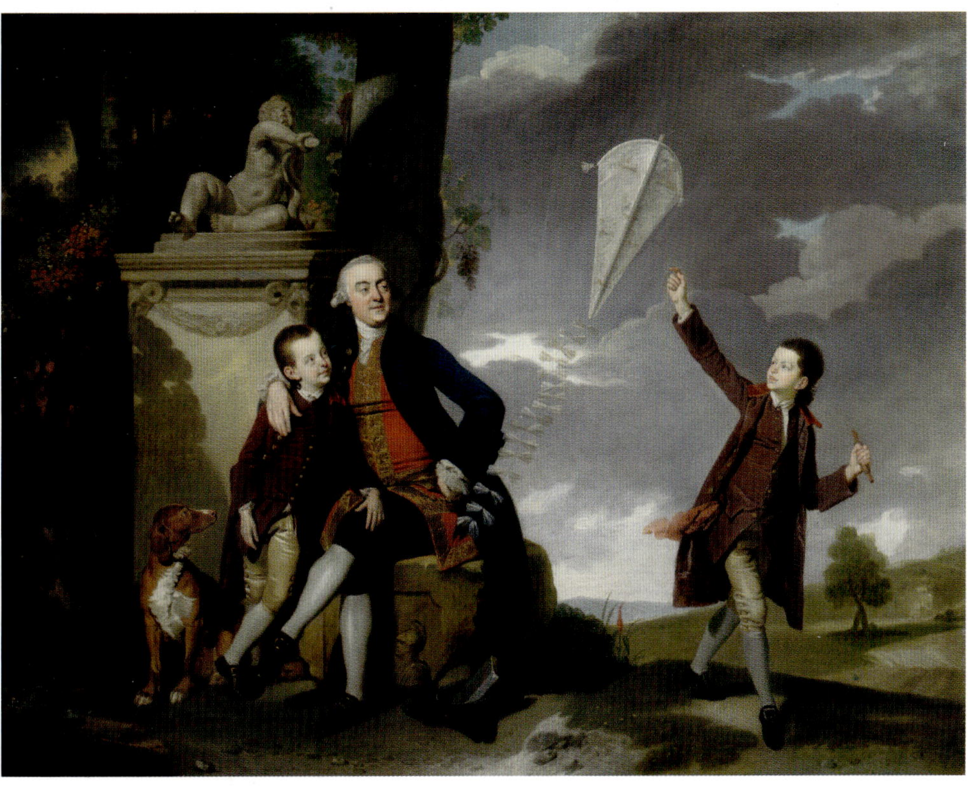

◄ **William Hogarth**

London, 1697–1764

Portrait of the Mackinen Children, 1747

Oil on canvas, 180 x 143 cm
Bequeathed, Sir Hugh Lane, 1918
NGI.791

During the 1740s Hogarth produced a number of large-scale portraits to demonstrate that he was worthy of the esteem of the leading artists of the day, and to prove he was not simply a painter and engraver of satirical subjects. He painted Elizabeth Mackinen and her brother William while they were briefly in London, probably to complete their education (they lived in Antigua). Hogarth includes symbolic objects such as the sunflower, the butterfly, the shells in the girl's lap and the boy's book to suggest that these children must soon choose between the transitory and the more enduring things of life.

▲ **Johan Zoffany**

Frankfurt am Main 1733–1810 Kew, London

Portrait of George Fitzgerald with his Sons George and Charles, c.1764

Oil on canvas, 98.5 x 123.5 cm
Heritage Gift, John and Bernie Gallagher, 2007
NGI.2007.76

The German-born Johan Zoffany was regarded as the finest painter of the conversation piece in England in the 1760s and received commissions from many distinguished families. George Fitzgerald, who had served as a captain in the Austrian army, is shown seated on a stone pedestal, upon which a Roman soldier is carved, which may be a reference to his military career. His son George, shown flying a kite, became a gambler who was involved in several disputes and was later convicted of murder and hanged. Fitzgerald's other son, Charles, standing beside his father, led a less eventful life and inherited the family estate in County Mayo.

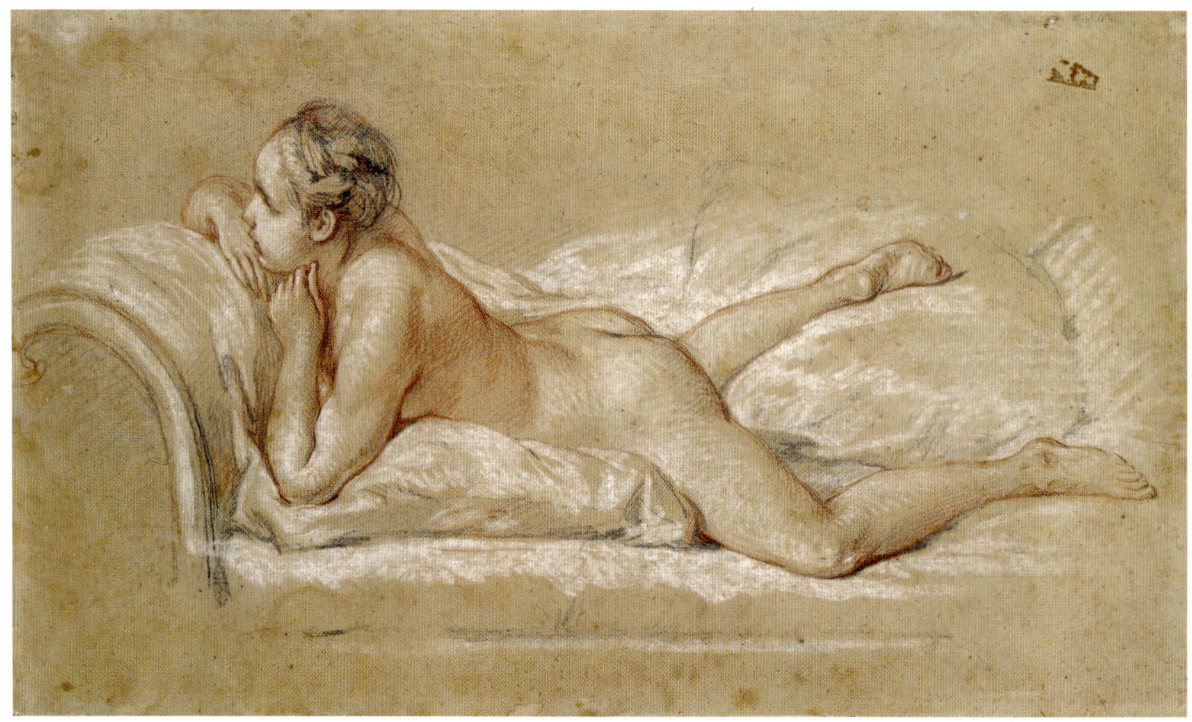

▲ **François Boucher**

Paris, 1703–1770

A Female Nude Reclining on a Chaise-Longue, c.1752

Graphite, red and white chalk on brown paper,
22.2 x 36.2 cm
Purchased, 2007
NGI.2007.3

François Boucher's sensuous images of women typify the French Rococo style. Tradition has it that the model for this provocatively posed nude is Marie-Louise O'Murphy, a young courtesan of Irish descent who became a mistress of Louis XV. She is known to have modelled for Boucher, who became first painter to the king and who also worked for his famous mistress Madame de Pompadour. This drawing has a fresh immediacy, suggesting it was drawn from life. The erotic pose is similar to that in Boucher's painting *The Blonde Odalisque* (1752; Alte Pinakothek, Munich).

▸ **Antonio Canova**

Possagno 1757–1822 Venice

Amorino, 1789–1791

Marble, 141 cm
Heritage Gift, Bank of Ireland, 1998
NGI.8358

Canova was the most talented and innovative sculptor of the Neo-classical period. His studio in Rome became a meeting place for intellectuals, collectors and tourists. In 1789 he was visited by the Irishman John David La Touche, who commissioned this statue. Canova idealised the body of the adolescent boy personifying Cupid or, as he was known in Italian, Amorino, achieving an elegant, classical simplicity. The smooth marble of the skin contrasts with the varied textures of hair, decorative bow and quiver. The sculpture was acquired by the Bank of Ireland and donated to the Gallery in honour of the philanthropic La Touche family, first governors of the bank.

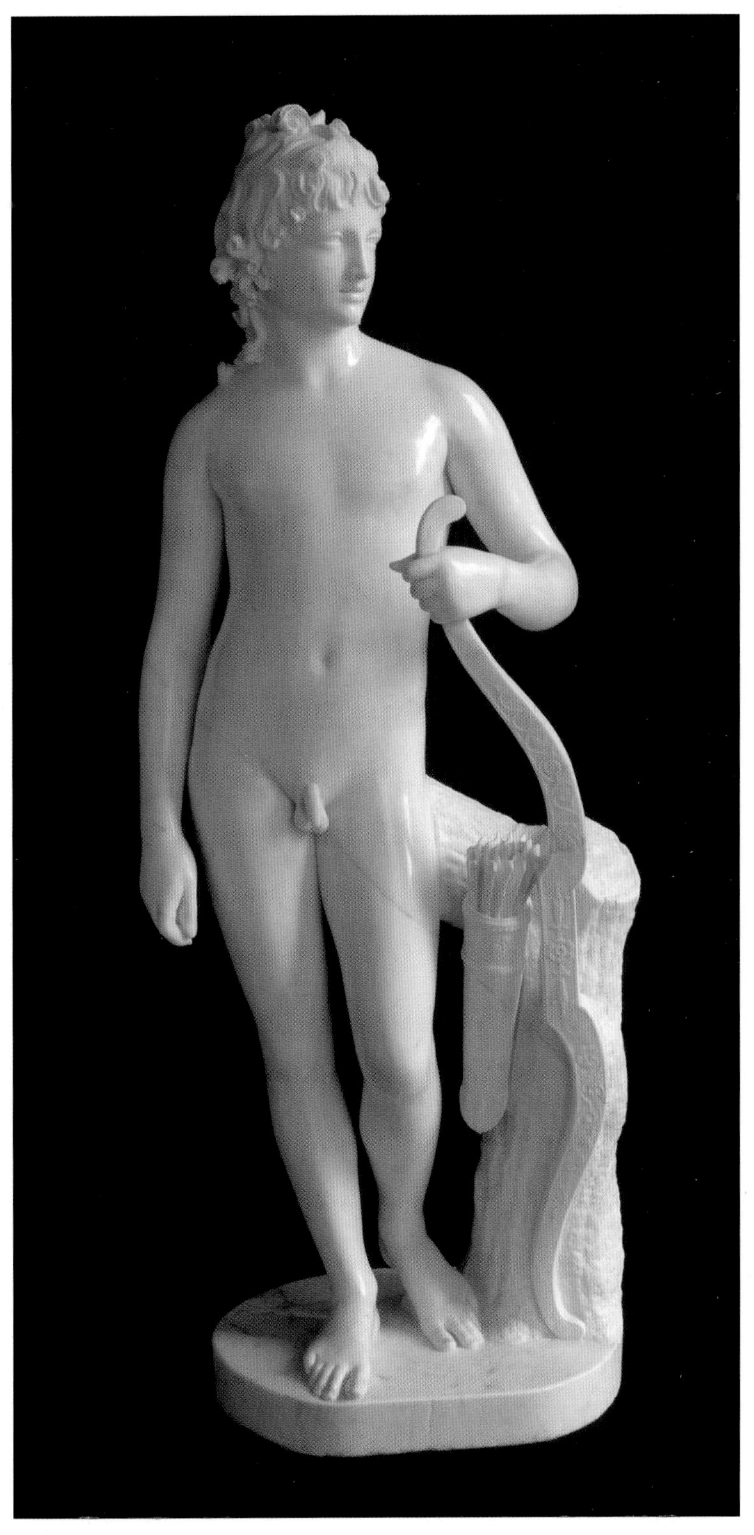

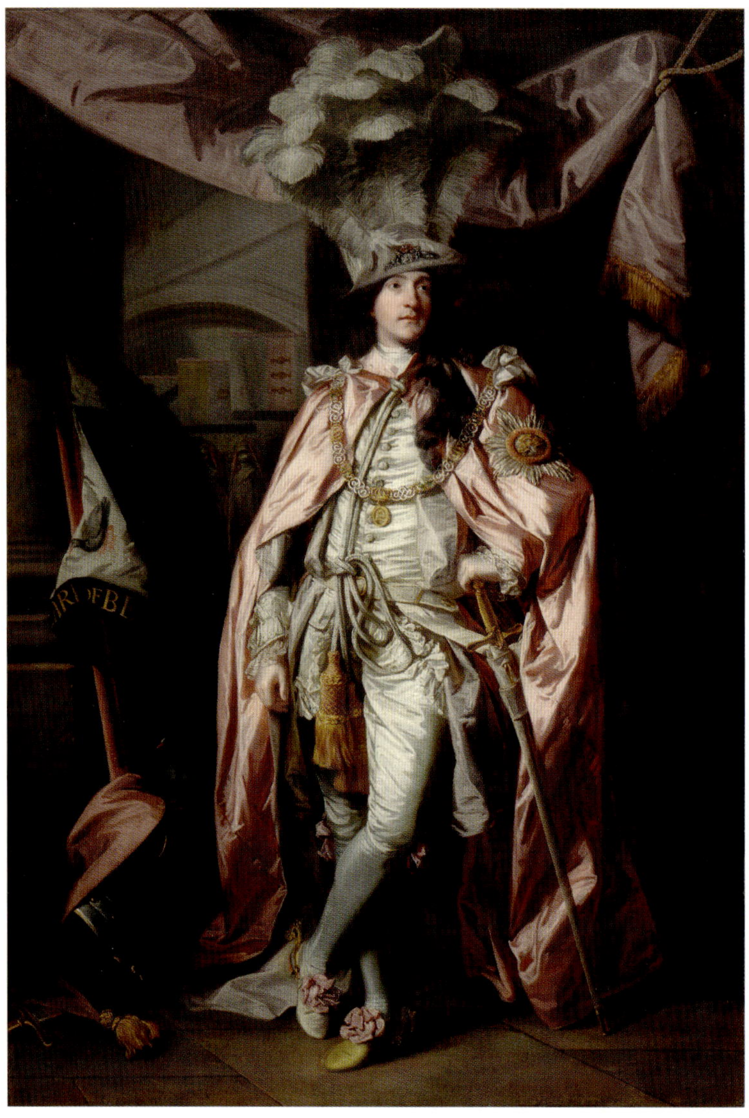

Joshua Reynolds

Plympton 1723–1792 London

Portrait of Charles Coote, 1st Earl of Bellamont (1738–1800), in Robes of the Order of the Bath, 1773–1774

Oil on canvas, 245 x 162 cm
Purchased, 1875
NGI.216

During the 1760s Charles Coote served as MP for County Cavan and was made a Knight of the Bath, an order that rewarded political and military service. Coote was known for his pomposity and vanity, and was the only Knight of the Bath painted in such a flamboyant pose and actually wearing the Order's ostrich-plumed hat (which would normally be placed on a table). His ceremonial satin cloak is complemented by shoes sporting rosettes and spurs. Reynolds, then the leading British portrait painter and first President of the Royal Academy, has added a note of humour by including a live coot perched beneath an embroidered banner, in reference to his patron's name.

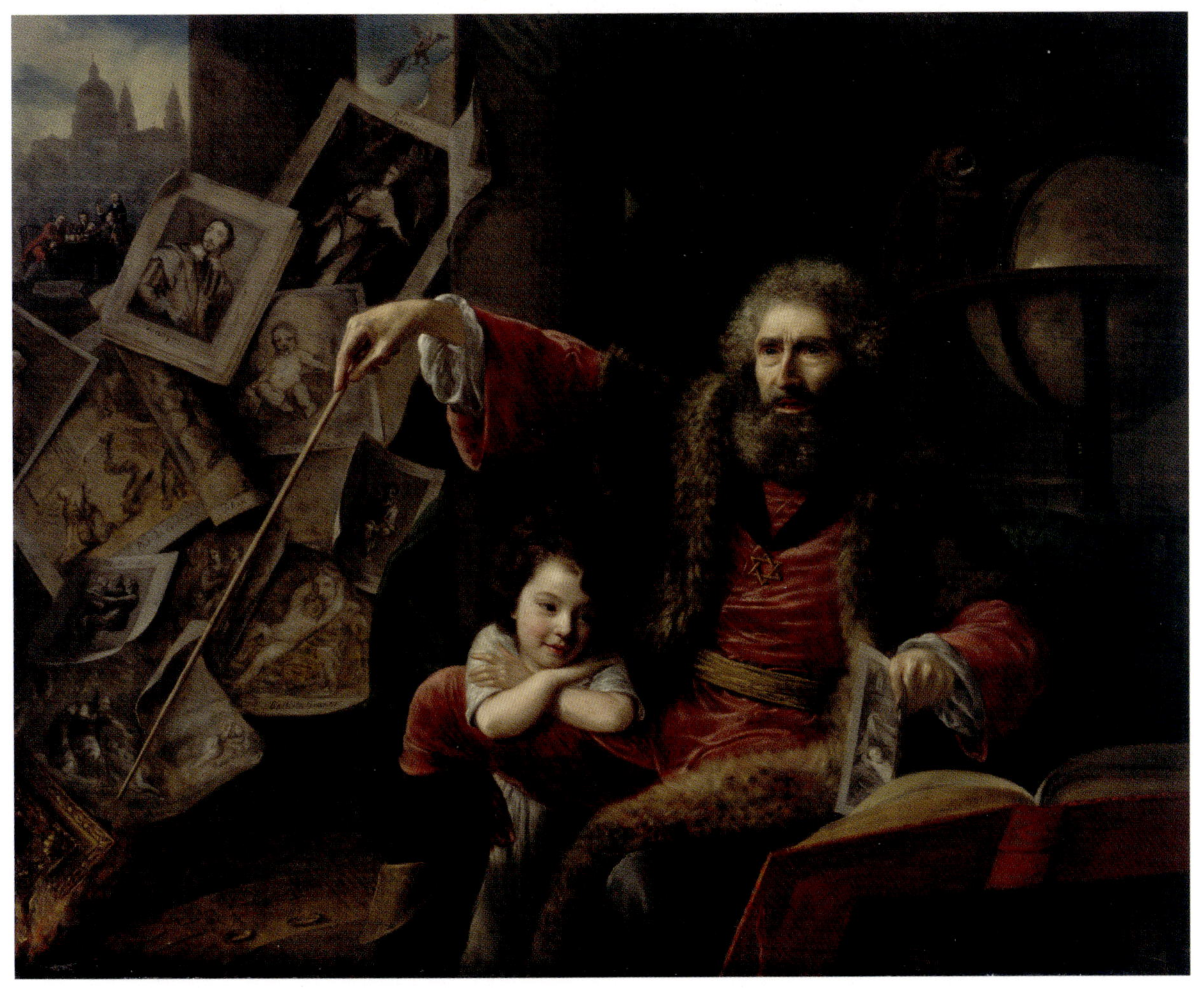

Nathaniel Hone the Elder

Dublin 1718–1784 London

The Conjuror, 1775

Oil on canvas, 145 x 173 cm
Purchased, 1966 (Shaw Fund)
NGI.1790

This picture was an audacious attack on Joshua Reynolds, one of the most revered artistic figures of his generation. Hone regarded Reynolds's reliance on the art of Old Masters in his own practice as mere plagiarism. In the picture, a magician conjures a painting from Old Master prints delivered by a winged demon. The painting was excluded from the Royal Academy annual exhibition on the erroneous grounds that other details were intended to offend the academician Angelica Kauffman. In response Hone installed the painting in a rival show, the first solo exhibition of its kind in London.

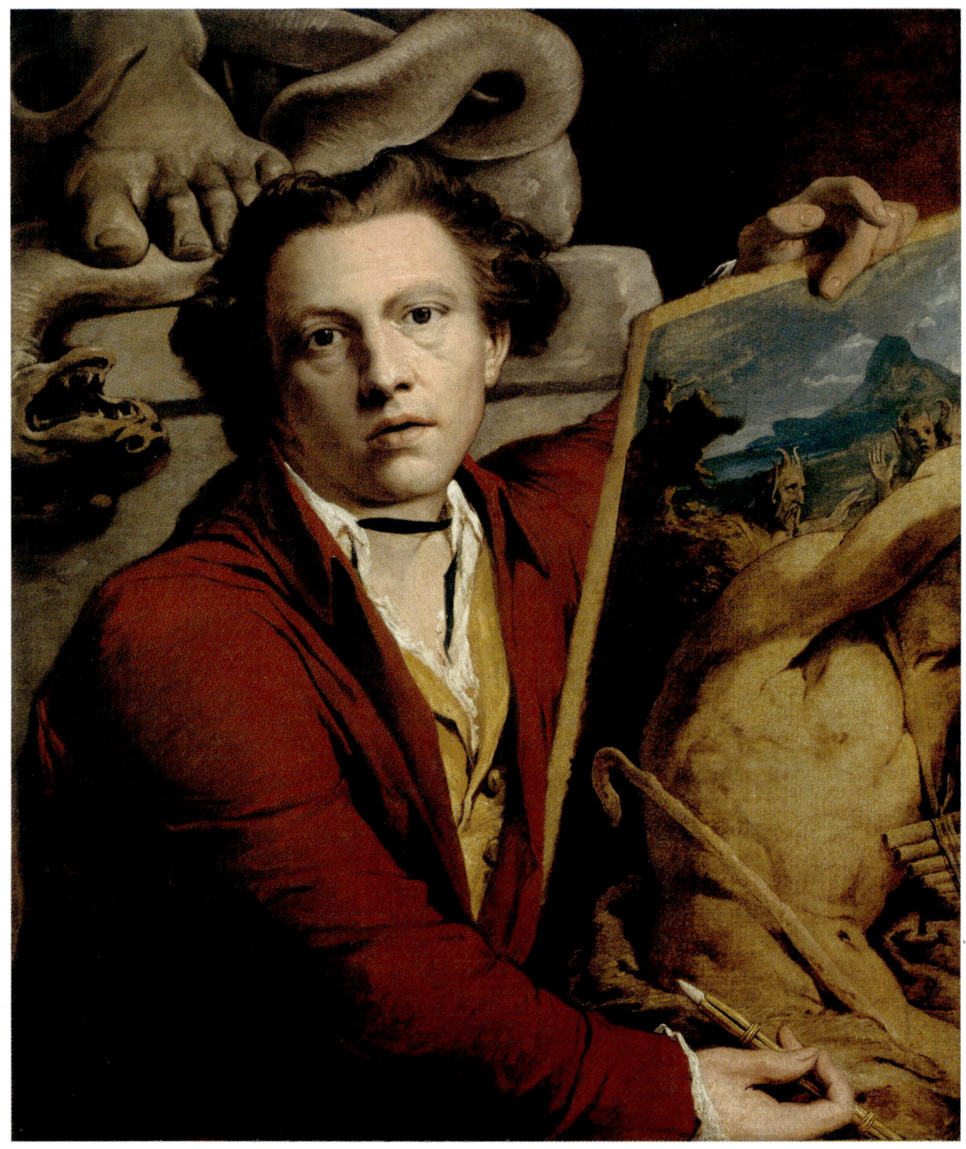

James Barry

Cork 1741–1806 London

Self-portrait as Timanthes,
c.1780–1803

Oil on canvas, 76 x 63 cm
Purchased, 1934
NGI.971

Barry initially used this portrait, derived from a classical text, in 1780 as the source for his representation of Timanthes in a mural at the Society of Arts in London. Over 20 years later, when invited by the Society to provide a self-portrait for reproduction, he proposed the same image. In the picture he holds aloft a painting in which satyrs gaze in fear at a Cyclops. Barry's deliberate placement of himself between this painting and a statue of Hercules crushing the serpent of Envy was intended to reflect his perseverance in the face of adversity.

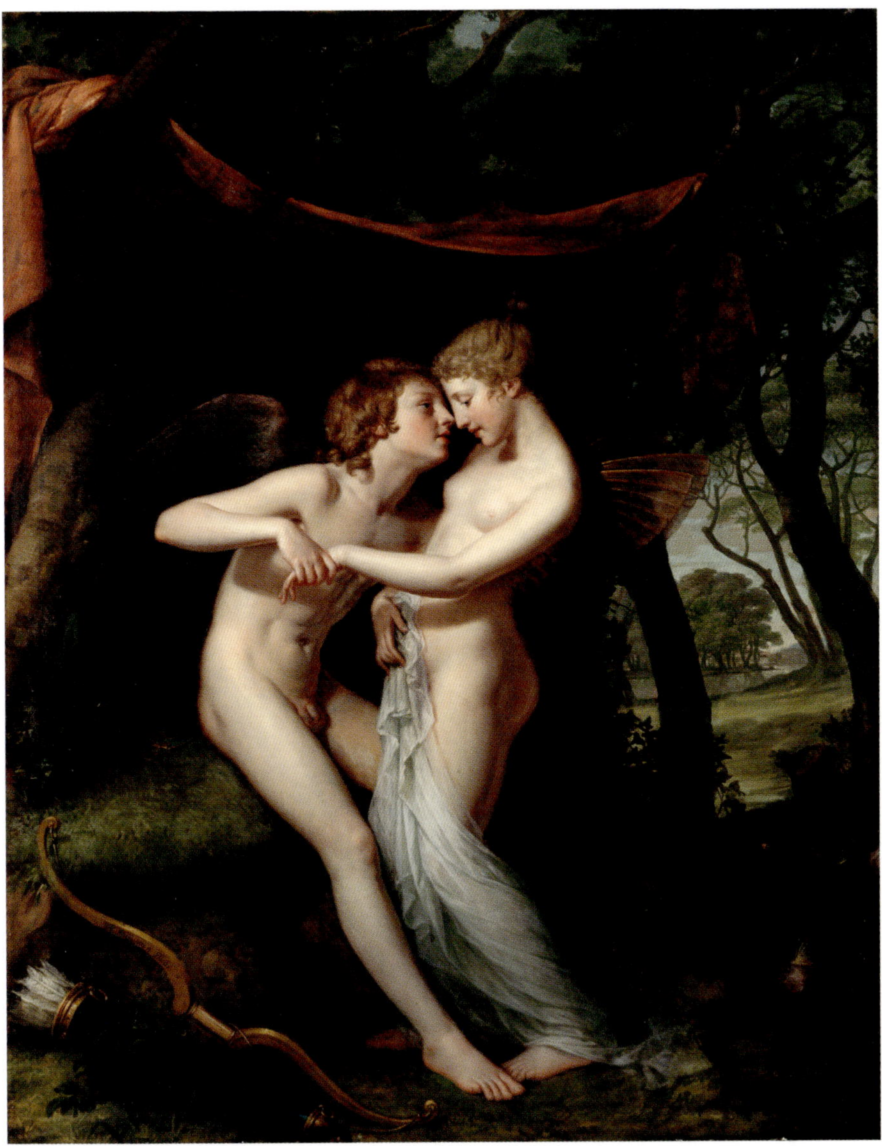

Hugh Douglas Hamilton

Dublin, 1740–1808

Cupid and Psyche in the Nuptial Bower, 1792–1793

Oil on canvas, 198 x 151 cm
Presented, Friends of the National Collections of Ireland, 1956
NGI.1342

This painting was influenced by antique sculptures in the Capitoline Museum in Rome and the Uffizi Gallery in Florence, as well as by a sculpture of the same subject by Hamilton's friend Antonio Canova. The classical tale of Cupid and Psyche came to be read as an allegory for voyages of the soul on earth and union with the divine after death. The butterfly was a symbol of the soul and of Psyche in Greek art, while the rose, bow and quiver are attributes of Cupid. The ivy growing in the background, meanwhile, represents immortality.

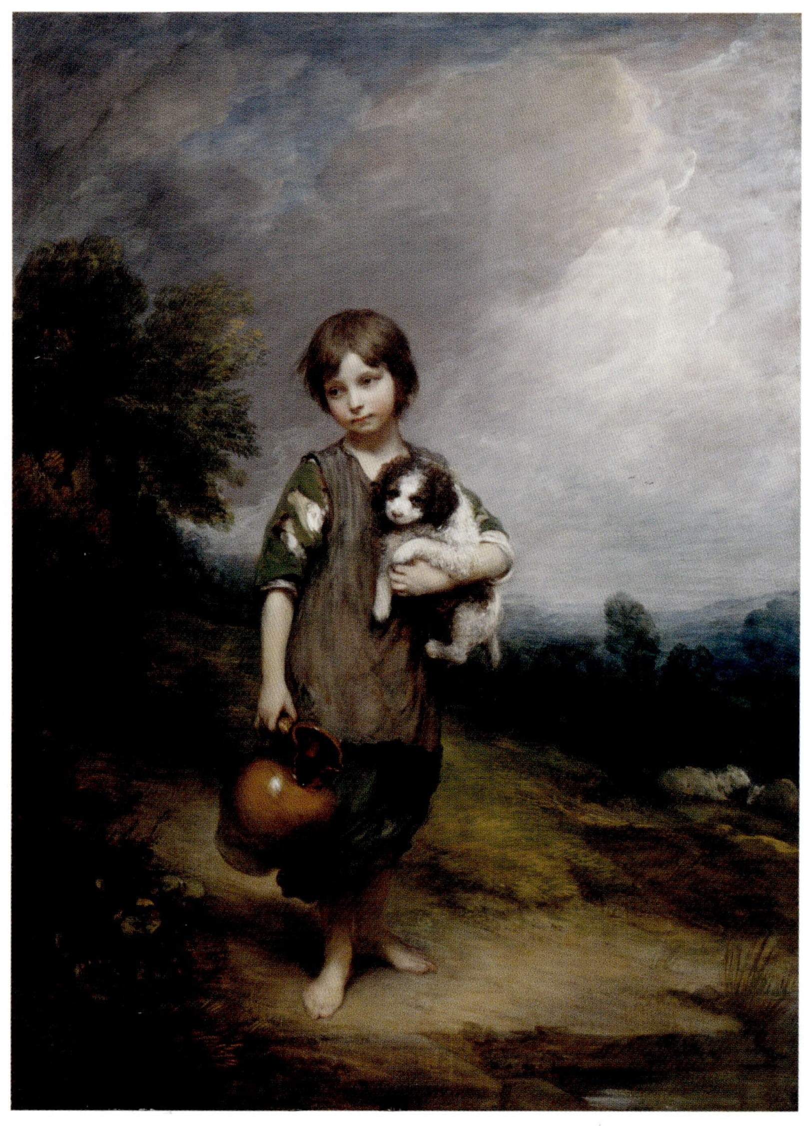

Thomas Gainsborough

Sudbury 1727–1788 London

The Cottage Girl, 1785

Oil on canvas, 174 x 124.5 cm
Presented, Sir Alfred and Lady Beit, 1987
(Beit Collection)
NGI.4529

A child in ragged clothing has come from a cottage to take water from a brook. She holds a broken earthenware pitcher in one hand and a dog in the other. Gainsborough demonstrates his personal response to the predicament of poor children but makes no moral point in this work. During the 1780s he painted almost 20 such 'fancy pictures' of rustic figures, often children, set in imaginary landscapes. These emotive works struck a deep chord with the British public, appealing to the contemporary taste for picturesque idylls.

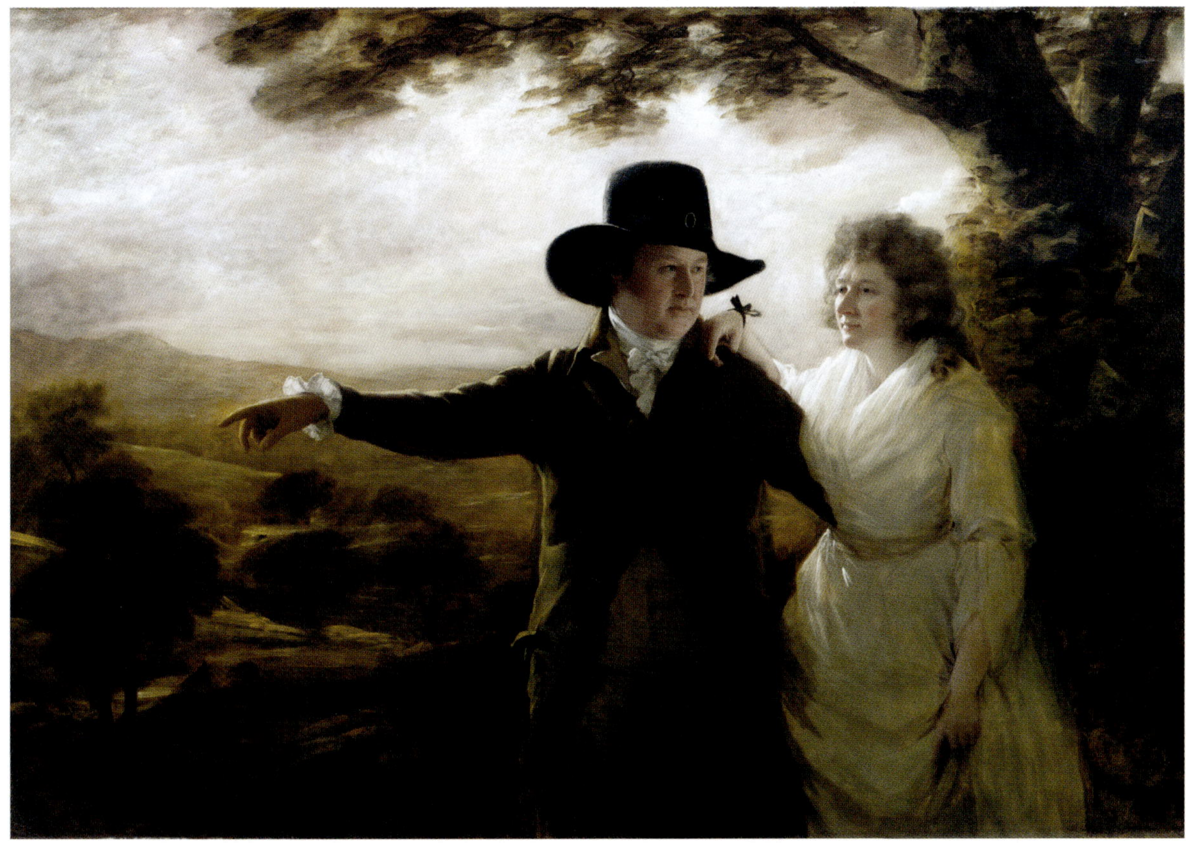

Henry Raeburn
Stockbridge 1756–1823 Edinburgh
Portrait of Sir John and Lady Clerk of Penicuik, 1791

Oil on canvas, 145 x 206 cm
Presented, Sir Alfred and Lady Beit, 1987
(Beit Collection)
NGI.4530

Sir John Clerk was a descendant of a rich merchant who had built Penicuik House in the Pentland hills, near Edinburgh. He married Rosemary Dacre from Cumberland, and their close relationship is beautifully conveyed in this double portrait by Henry Raeburn, the leading Scottish painter of the late eighteenth century. As Sir John indicates his estate to his wife, their figures integrate with the landscape through his gesture and Raeburn's treatment of natural light, which falls on Lady Clerk's face and dress. Raeburn created a series of large, informal portraits set in outdoor locations suffused in golden light, among which this work is a masterpiece.

1800–1900

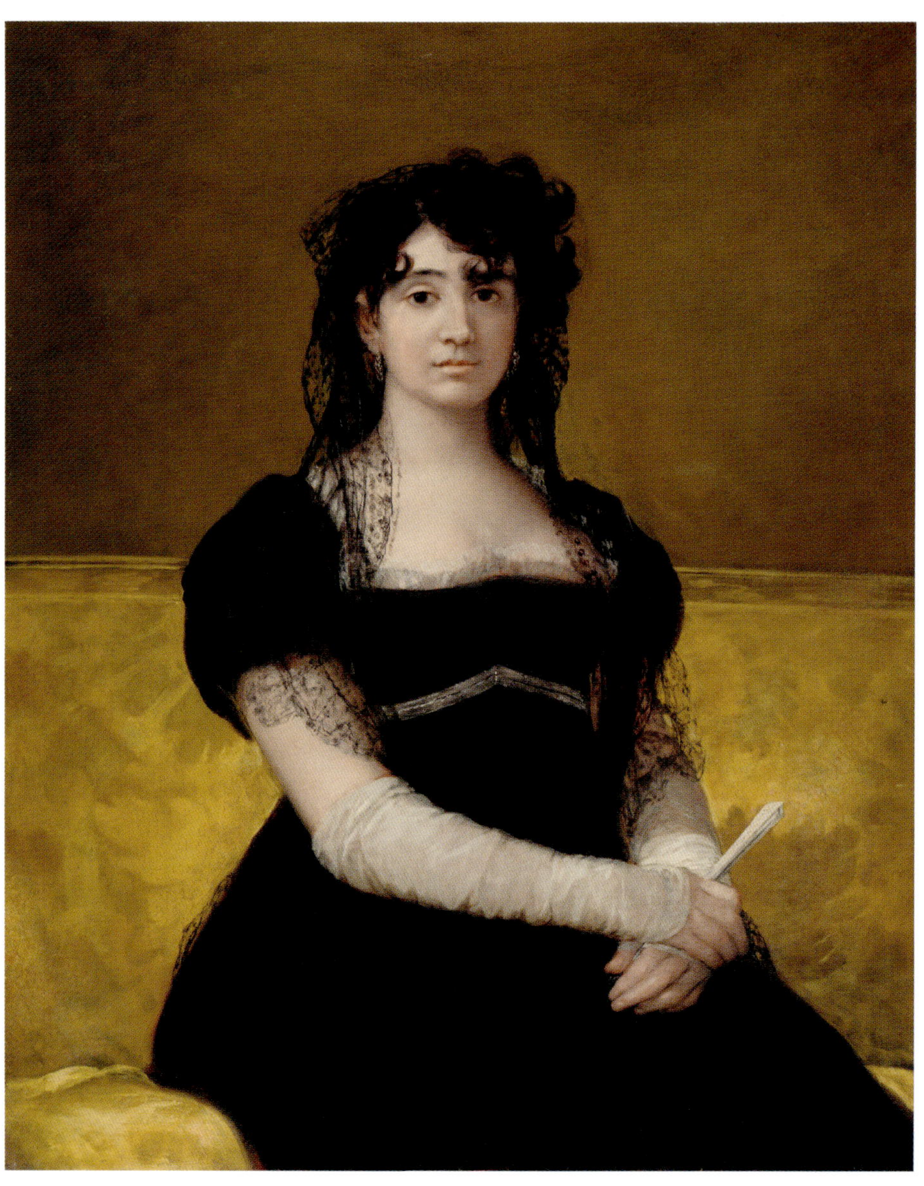

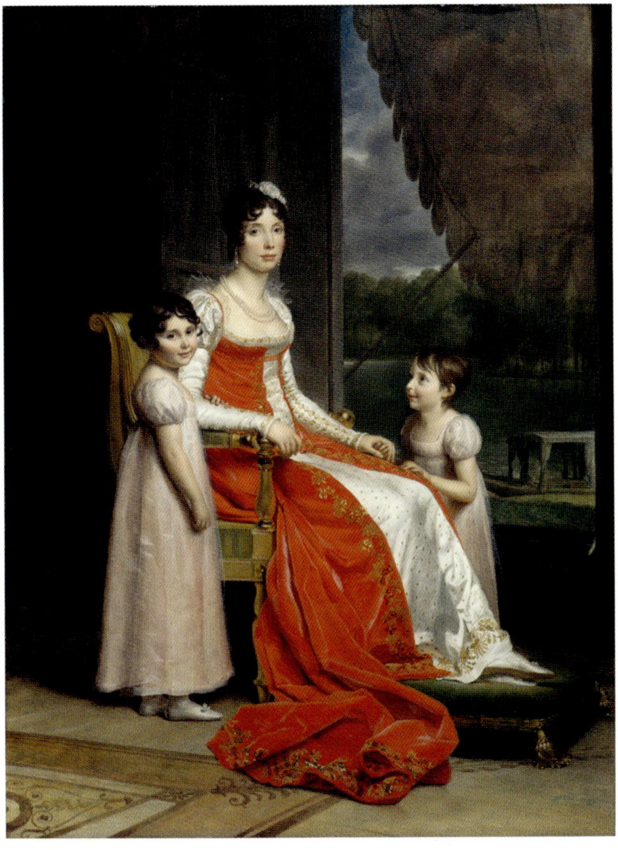

◄ **Francisco José de Goya y Lucientes**

Fuendetodos 1746–1828 Bordeaux

Portrait of Doña Antonia Zárate, c.1805

Oil on canvas, 103.5 x 82 cm
Presented, Sir Alfred and Lady Beit, 1987
(Beit Collection)
NGI.4539

Doña Antonia Zárate was one of several stage personalities whom Goya painted. In this striking portrait he accentuates the actress's dark beauty by contrasting her black empire-line gown and lace mantilla against a yellow damask settee. In Madrid, Goya became court painter to King Charles III; his career prospered and he acquired many distinguished patrons. He was mainly known as a portraitist but he also painted religious, historical, political and genre subjects and was an accomplished printmaker.

▲ **Baron François Gérard**

Rome 1770–1837 Paris

Julie Bonaparte as Queen of Spain with her Daughters, Zénaïde and Charlotte, 1808–1809

Oil on canvas, 199 x 142 cm
Purchased, 1972 (Shaw Fund)
NGI.4055

As principal portraitist to Napoleon I, Gérard created many portraits of the emperor and his family. Marie-Julie Clary was the wife of Napoleon's brother Joseph, who in 1808 became King of Spain. Julie is portrayed here as his queen, wearing a ceremonial white satin empire-line gown with gold lamé foliage at the hemline, a detail which is repeated on her red velvet over-cape. Her daughters Zénaïde (b. 1801) and Charlotte (b. 1802) wear pink muslin and voile dresses. The elegant Neo-classical interior is thought to be that of the Château of Mortefontaine.

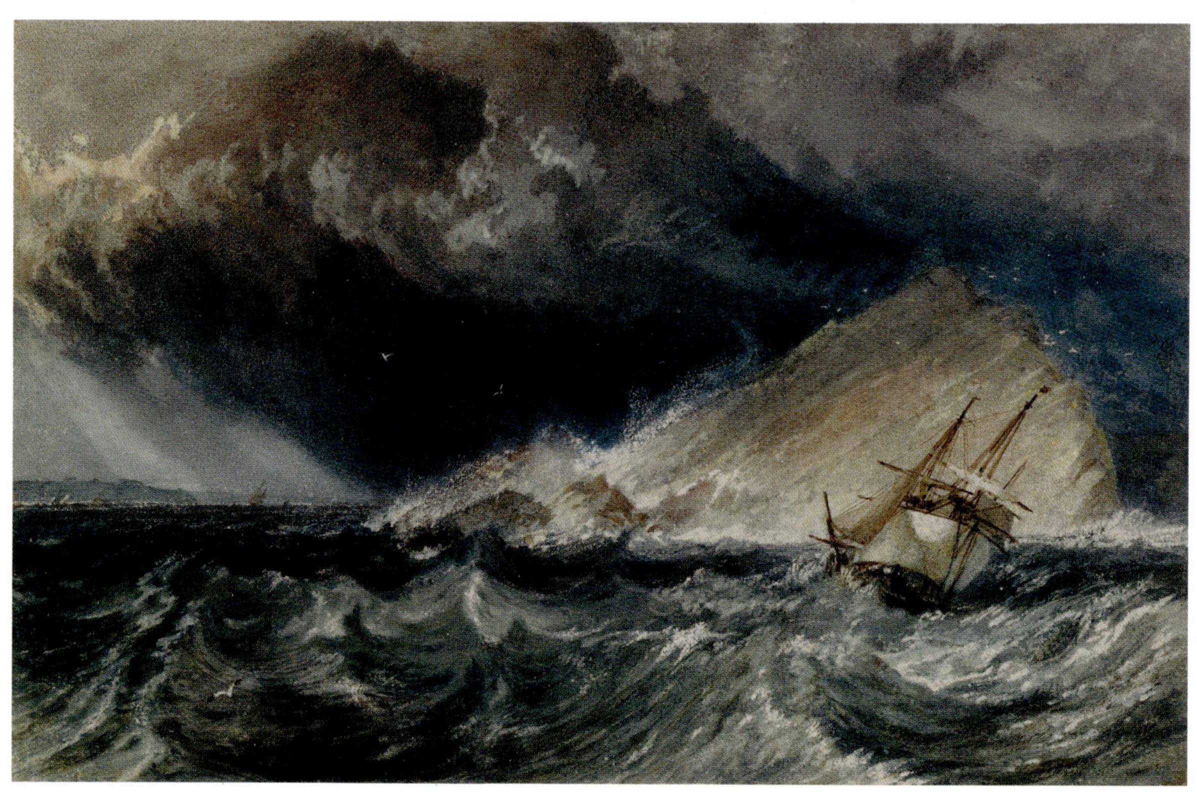

Joseph Mallord William Turner

London, 1775–1851

A Ship against the Mewstone, at the Entrance to Plymouth Sound, c.1814

Watercolour with white highlights and scraping-out on cream wove card, 15.6 x 23.7 cm
Bequeathed, Henry Vaughan, 1900
NGI.2413

Joseph Mallord William Turner is famed as one of the most groundbreaking British landscape artists of the nineteenth century. Between 1811 and 1815 he produced a series of watercolour scenes for William Cooke's (1775–1858) print series *Picturesque Views of the Southern Coast of England*. This view appeared as a black and white print in 1815 in part six of the series. The ship, probably a Royal Naval vessel, is dwarfed by the dreaded Mewstone which lies in Plymouth Sound off Wembury Bay. During the summer of 1813 Turner spent time travelling along the coast making studies for this series.

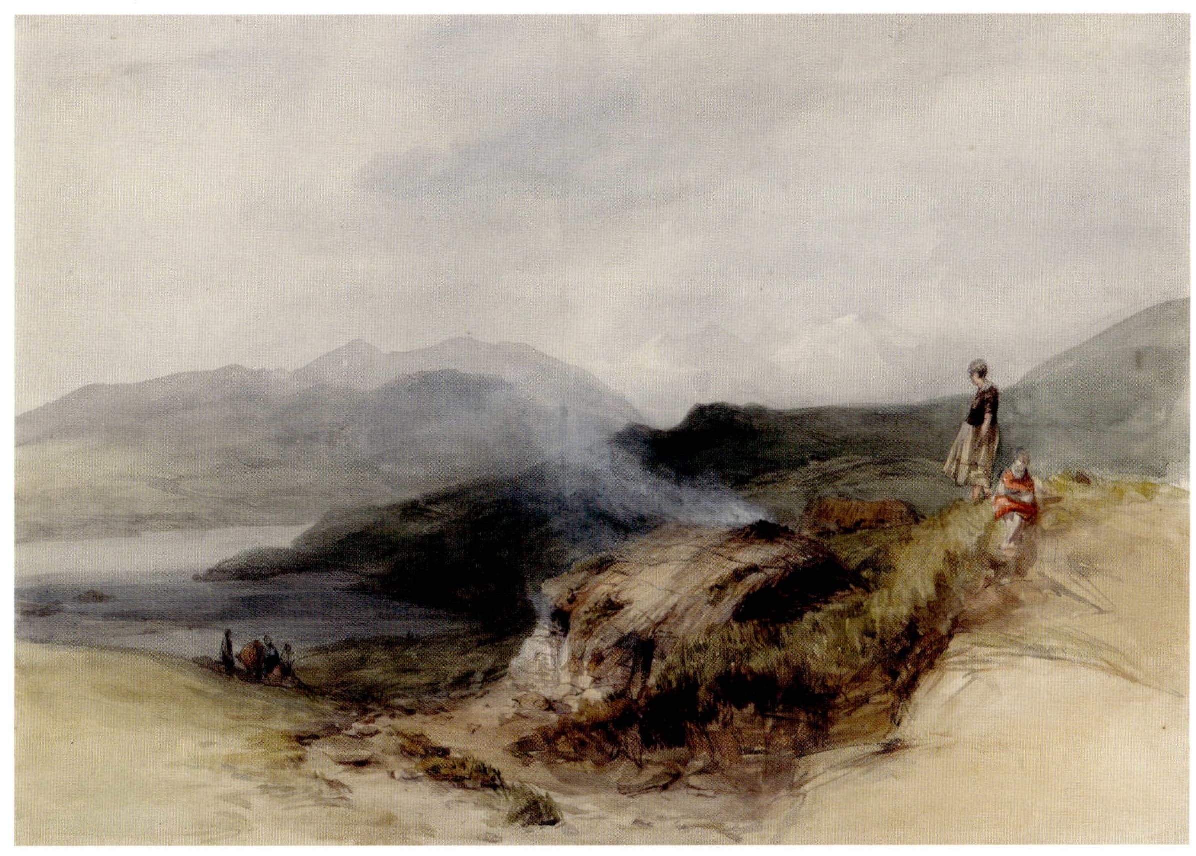

William Evans of Eton

Eton, 1798–1877

Killary, near the Mouth of the Bundoracha River, County Galway, 1838

Watercolour, graphite and glazes on paper, 42 x 58.5 cm
Purchased, 2008
NGI.2008.36.9

Evans was for many years the drawing master at Eton, the famous English public school. In 1835 and 1838 he toured Ireland and some of his west of Ireland studies were used as illustrations for Mr and Mrs Samuel C. Hall's 1843 guide book, *Ireland: its Scenery, Character &c.* This image of a simple thatched cottage built into an earthen bank gives a real sense of what life was like for the ordinary people of Connemara who scratched a living from the poor soil before the Great Famine.

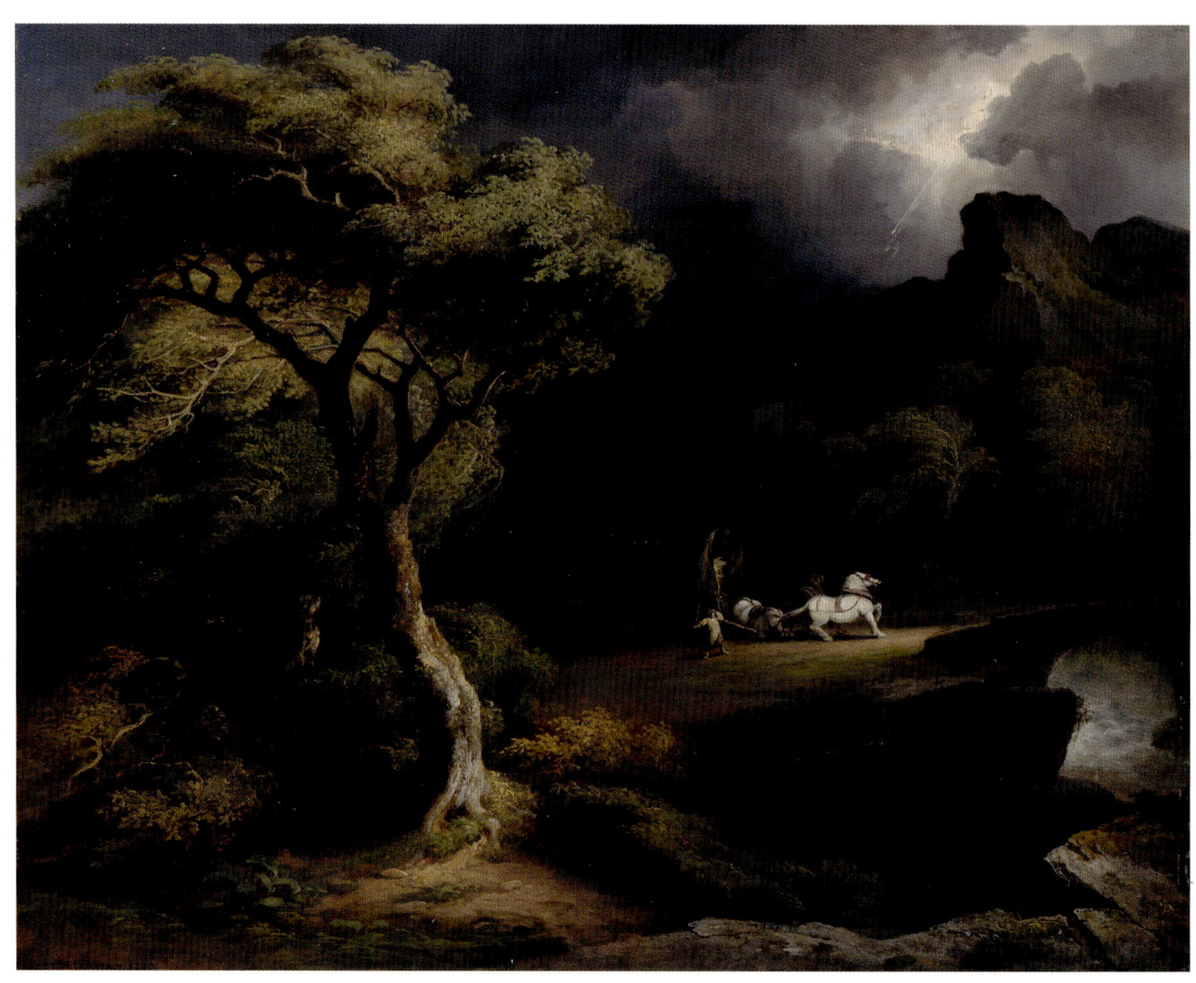

James Arthur O'Connor

Dublin 1792–1841 London

A Thunderstorm: the Frightened Wagoner, 1832

Oil on canvas, 63.7 x 76.7 cm
Presented, Mr F. McCormick, 1972
NGI.4041

This is one of O'Connor's finest works and a demonstration of his debt to Romanticism. While the meticulous detailing and harmonious palette is typical of O'Connor's work, the picture's drama contrasts starkly with the stillness that qualifies the artist's early landscapes. Among the painting's remarkable qualities is the manner in which it communicates, despite its diminutive size, the awesome and unpredictable power of nature. It has been suggested that the choice of subject was attributable to William Wordsworth's poem 'The Wagoner' of 1819 but nothing is known of O'Connor's literary preferences.

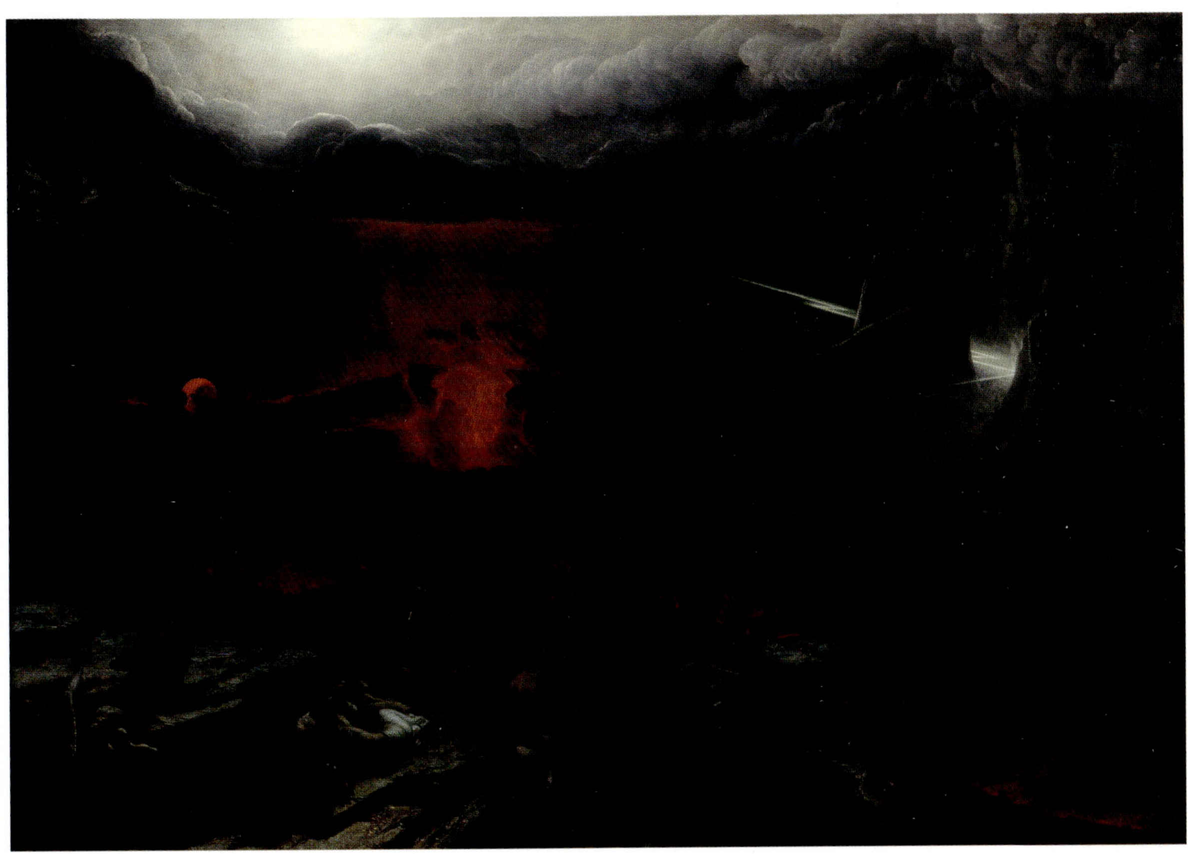

Francis Danby

Wexford 1793–1861 Exmouth

The Opening of the Sixth Seal, 1828

Oil on canvas, 185 x 255 cm
Purchased, 1871
NGI.162

This example of grand Romanticism illustrates a section from the Book of Revelations (6:12-17) in which, on the opening by God of the sixth seal on a scroll, the earth is torn apart and mankind descends into disarray. Danby's conspicuous departure from the biblical text is his inclusion of a crouching figure, similar to that adopted as the symbol of the Abolitionist movement, and a standing, liberated slave, who breaks the shackles around his wrists. The slave trade had been discontinued in 1807 in Britain but the bill for the abolition of slavery itself was not passed until 1833.

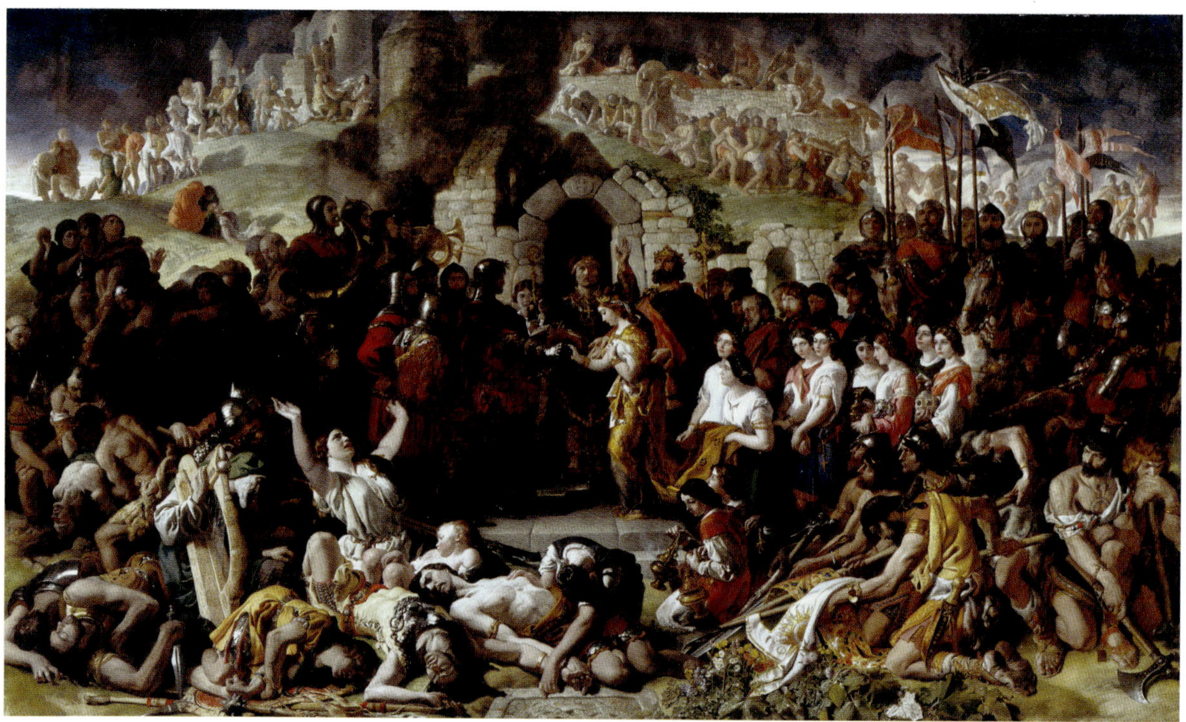

▲ **Daniel Maclise**

Cork 1806–1870 London

The Marriage of Strongbow and Aoife, c.1854

Oil on canvas, 315 x 513 cm
Presented, Sir Richard Wallace, 1879
NGI.205

The subject of this monumental and meticulously detailed picture is the marriage at Waterford in 1170 of the Norman military adventurer Richard de Clare, known as Strongbow, and the daughter of Dermot McMurrough, King of Leinster. The union has often been identified as representing the formal establishment of a Norman foothold in Ireland. Conceived for the decoration of the Palace of Westminster, the painting is an ambiguous representation of the victorious Normans and the vanquished Irish. Strongbow places his foot on a fallen Celtic cross, King Dermot looks on in alarm and an elderly musician slumps on his harp.

▶ **Frederic William Burton**

County Wicklow 1816–1900 London

Hellelil and Hildebrand, the Meeting on the Turret Stairs, 1864

Watercolour and gouache on paper, 95.5 x 60.8 cm
Bequeathed, Miss Margaret Stokes, 1900
NGI.2358

This watercolour was inspired by the medieval Danish ballad, *Hellelil and Hildebrand*, first translated into English by the artist's friend Whitley Stokes in 1855. It tells the story of Hellelil's love for her personal guard Hildebrand, whose murder is ordered by her disapproving father. Rather than illustrating a violent episode from this tragic story, Burton chooses to depict the ill-fated lovers in a tender, poignant embrace. The rich colour and romantic treatment of the subject matter echoes the work of the Pre-Raphaelites, whom Burton greatly admired. He worked slowly and carefully on his watercolours, often producing numerous preparatory studies, and used very fine brushstrokes, reminiscent of a miniaturist's technique.

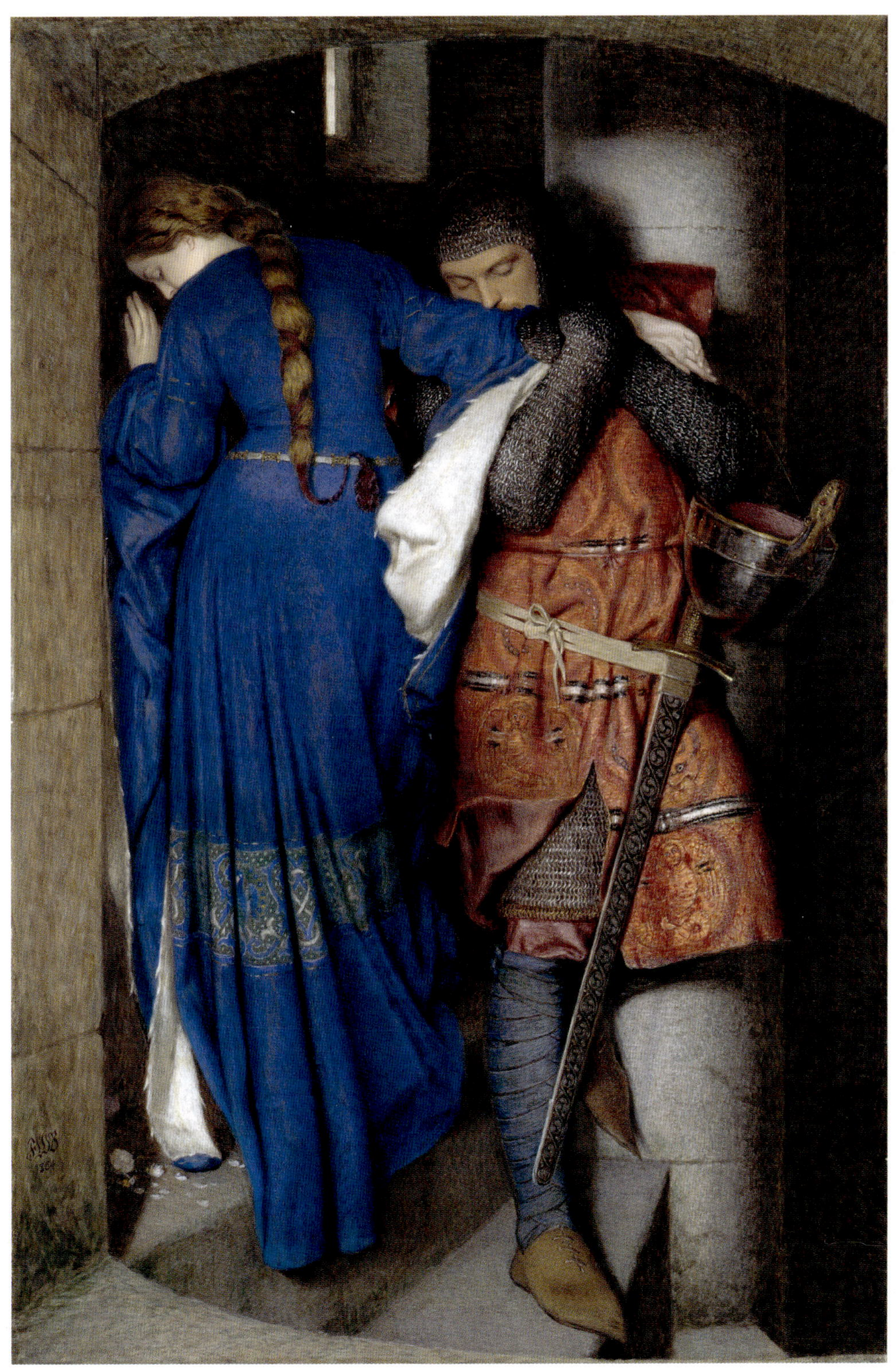

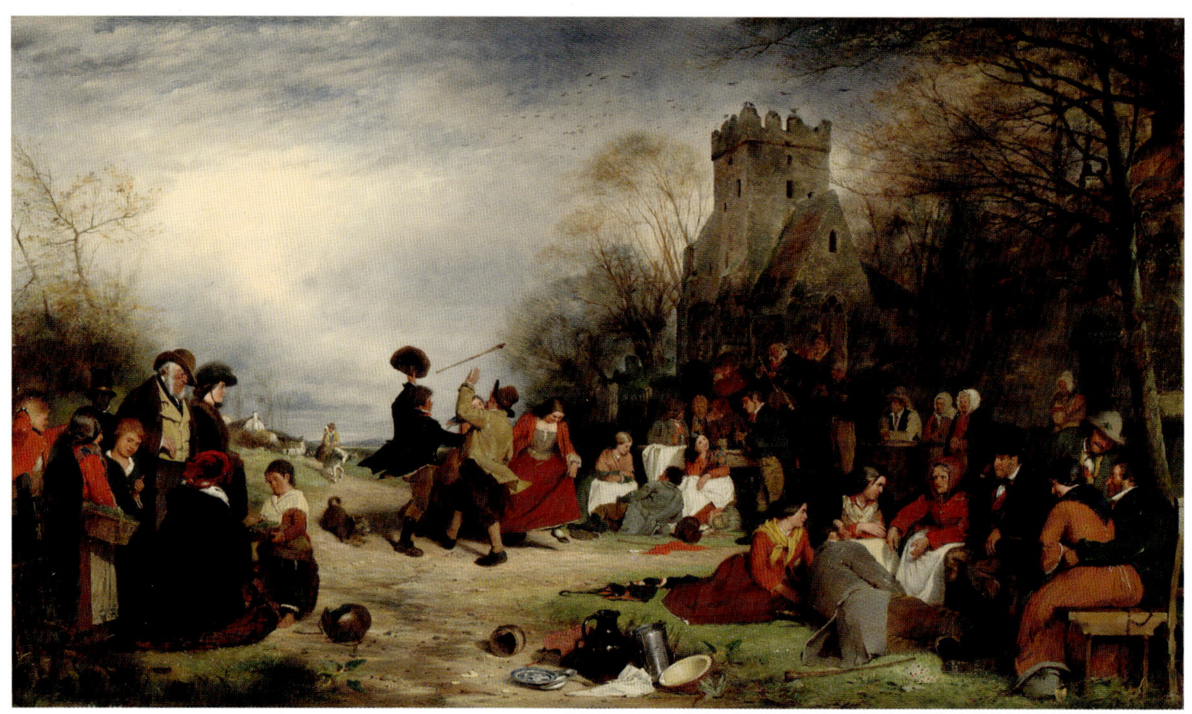

Erskine Nicol

Leith 1825–1904 Feltham

The 16th, 17th (St Patrick's Day), and 18th March, 1856

Oil on canvas, 79 x 131.7 cm
Purchased, 2008
NGI.2008.97

Though St Patrick's Day remained for most of the Irish population in the mid-nineteenth century principally an event in the liturgical calendar, Nicol depicts it here as an opportunity for commercial enterprise and revelry. This is emphasised by the fact that a woman to the right, enjoying the amorous approaches of a young man, sits on a set of rosary beads, while the church in the background is conspicuously shut. Nicol maintained a close and long-standing relationship with Ireland but is often associated with theatrical, and often pejorative, depictions of Irish peasants.

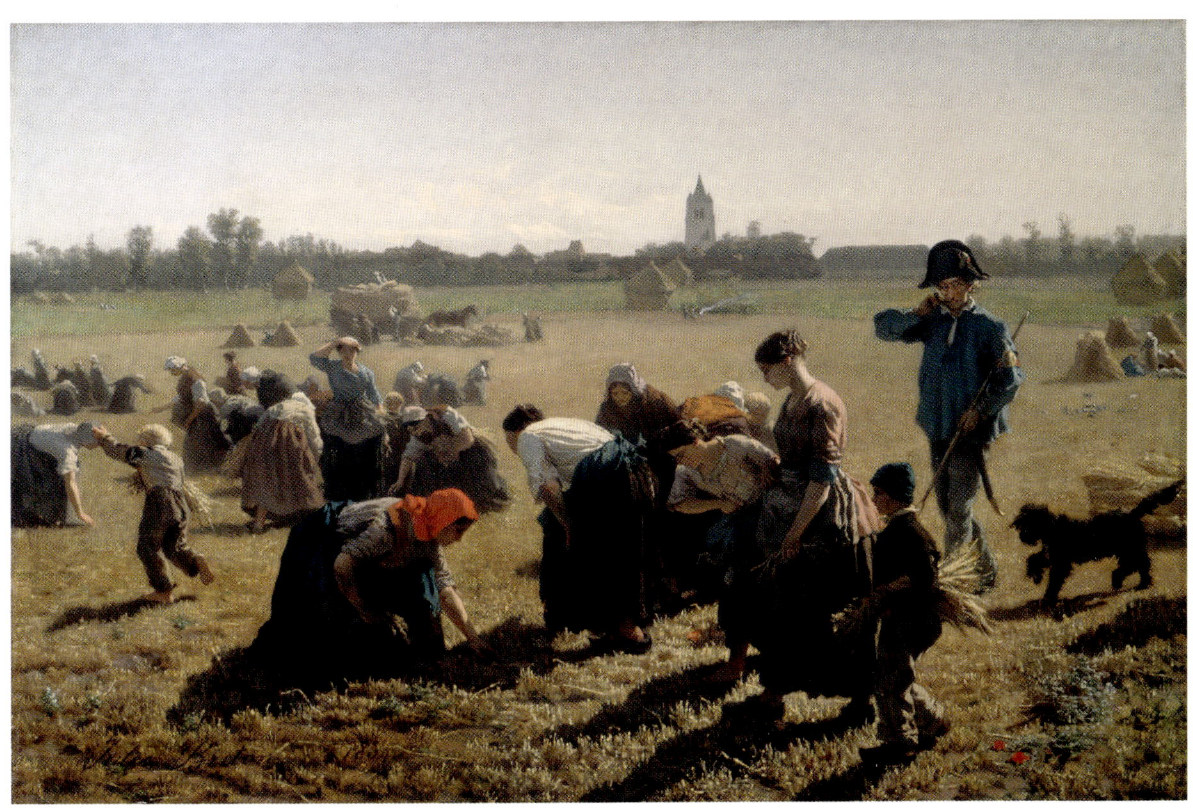

Jules Breton

Courrières 1827–1906 Paris

The Gleaners, 1854

Oil on canvas, 93 x 138 cm
Presented, Sir Alfred Chester Beatty, 1950
NGI.4213

Breton set this scene in his native village of Courrières, in the Artois region. It depicts women and children gathering the remnants of the harvest, under the supervision of a *garde-champêtre*. The model for the woman standing beside the small boy in the foreground was Elodie de Vigne, the daughter of Breton's art teacher. She and Breton married in 1858. Although he admired Gustave Courbet's bold realism, Breton preferred to depict the lives of the rural poor in a more idealised manner. His compositions are orderly, his figures classicised and his landscapes suffused with golden light.

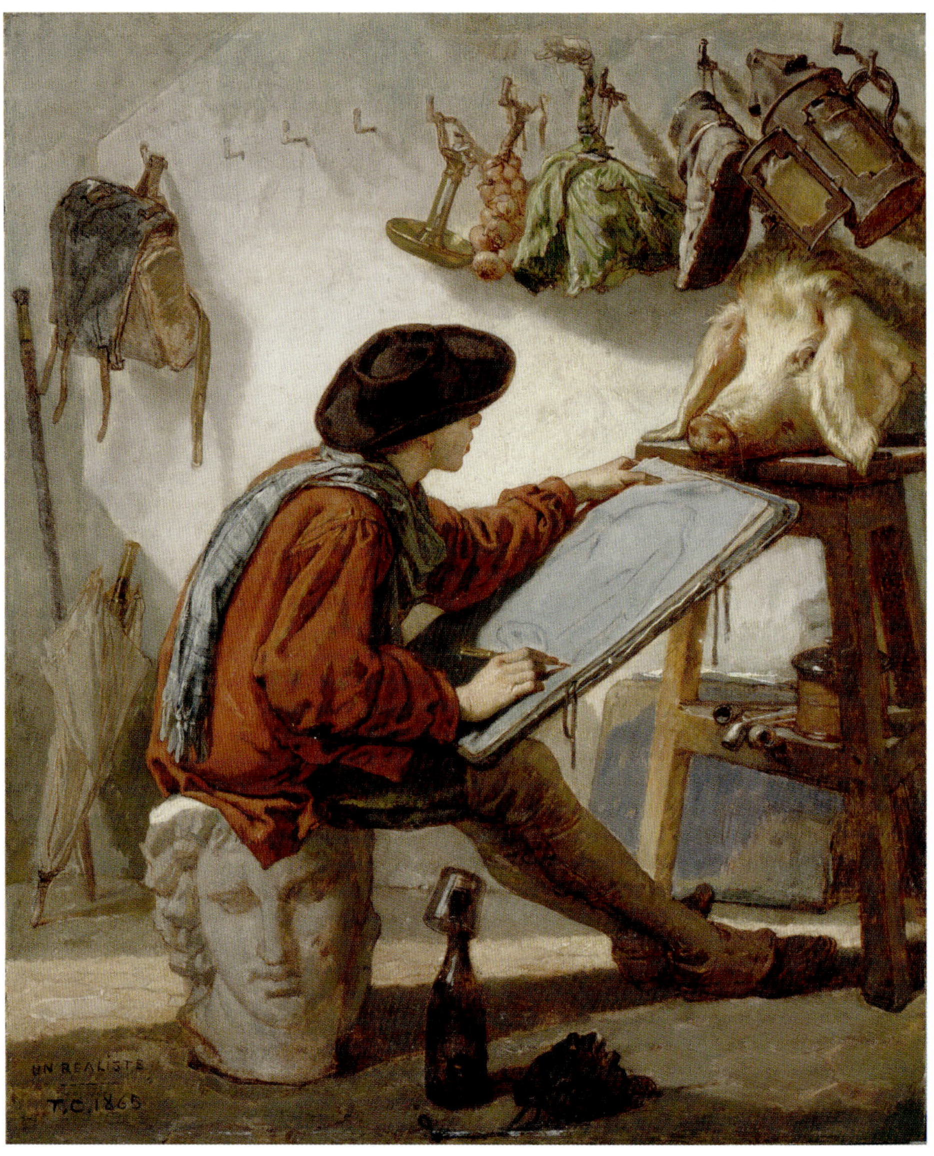

Thomas Couture

Senlis 1815–1879 Villiers-le-Bel

La Peinture Réaliste, 1865

Oil on panel, 56 x 45 cm
Presented, Sir Alfred Chester Beatty, 1950
NGI.4220

The history painter Thomas Couture ran a successful atelier in Paris during the 1850s. In this picture, he satirises the young artists who followed the Realist style pioneered by Gustave Courbet. These artists found inspiration in modern life rather than in historical or literary subjects. Here, a young painter sketches a pig's head. He sits on an antique cast, an indication of his disregard for historical art and for academic conventions. Mundane objects like the cabbage and boot hanging in the background reinforce this idea, while items such as the umbrella and knapsack suggest that he likes to paint en plein air.

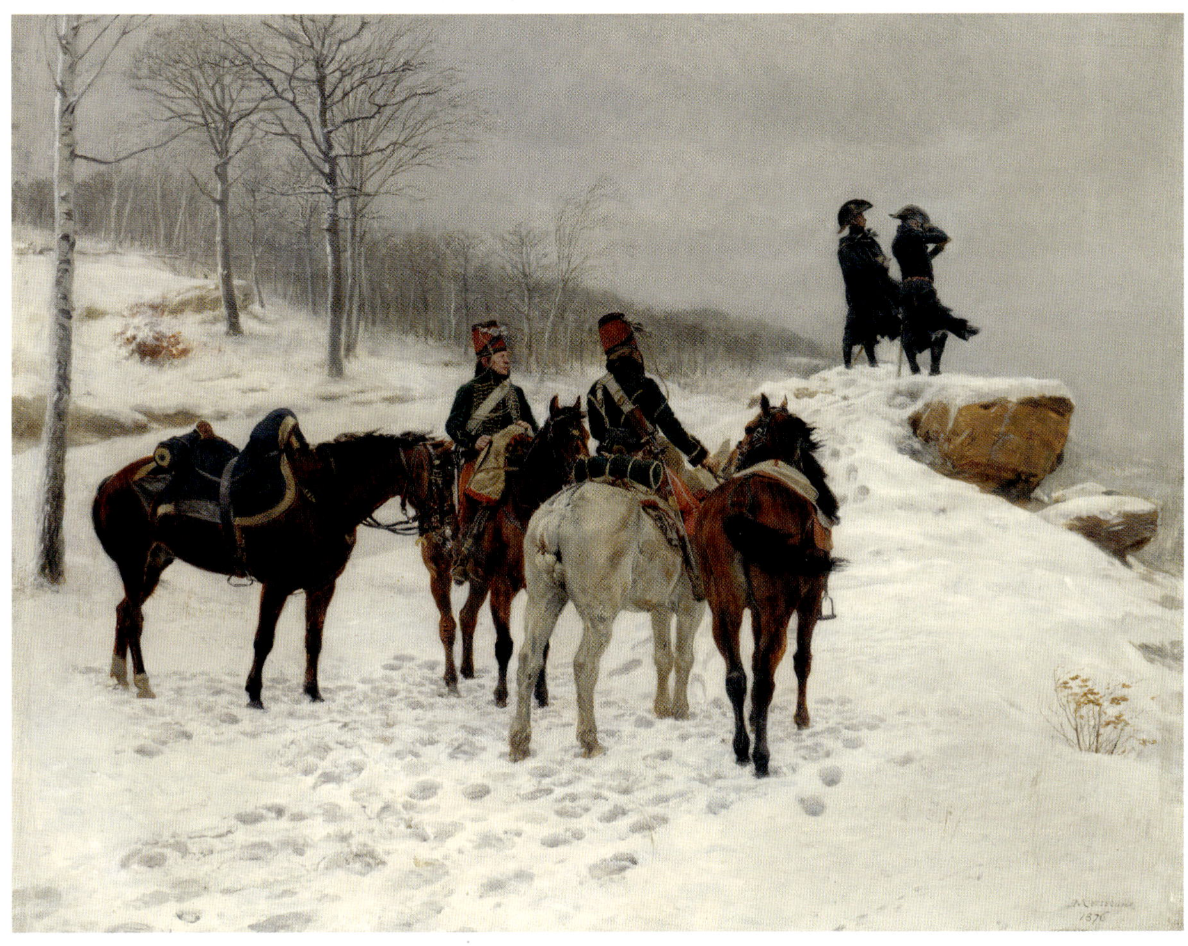

Jean-Louis Ernest Meissonier

Lyon 1815–1891 Poissy

Group of Cavalry in the Snow: Moreau and Dessoles before Hohenlinden, 1875

Oil on wood panel, 37.5 x 47 cm
Presented, Sir Alfred Chester Beatty, 1950
NGI.4263

Meissonier depicts the French general Victor Moreau planning strategy with his Chief of Staff, Dessoles, before his famous victory over the Austrians and Bavarians at Hohenlinden in 1800. The men stand on a promontory surveying the terrain, while two hussar troopers hold their horses. Meissonier was meticulous in researching his military scenes; he would borrow costumes, interview veterans, make models and even attempt to reconstruct the appearance of snowy battlefields with sugar and flour. He painted this work on panel, rather than canvas, in order to achieve a highly detailed finish.

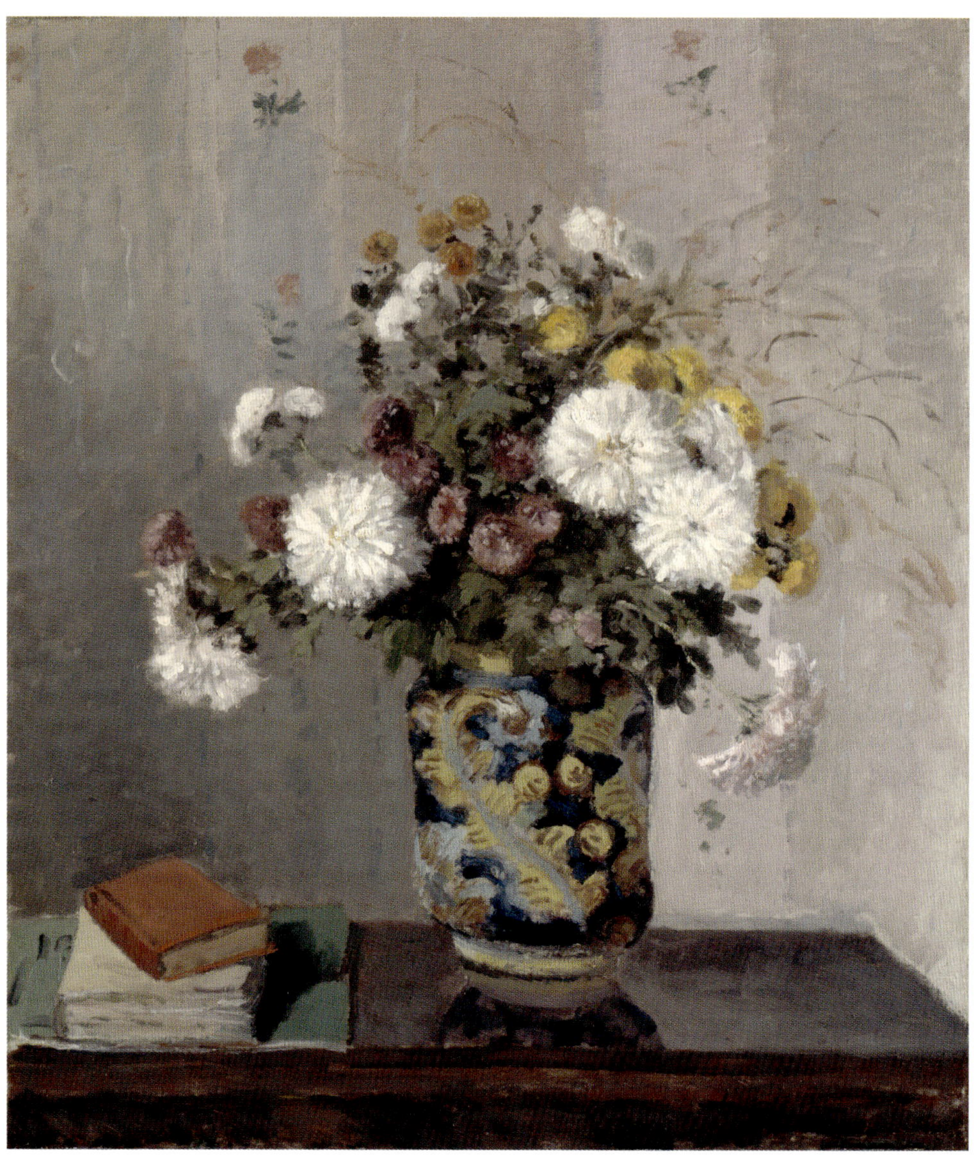

Camille Pissarro
Saint Thomas (Danish Virgin Islands)
1830–1903 Paris
Chrysanthemums in a Chinese Vase,
1873

Oil on canvas, 60 x 50.5 cm
Purchased, 1983 (Shaw Fund)
NGI.4459

Pissarro is often referred to as the 'Father of Impressionism'. Between 1872 and 1873 he painted a number of still lifes at his home in Pontoise. Several of these include the distinctive striped wallpaper seen in this work. Here, the reflection of the vase on the polished tabletop demonstrates Pissarro's interest in the effect of light on varied surfaces. Other Impressionists, including Monet and Renoir, also painted chrysanthemums. Not only were these flowers visually attractive but their associations with Japanese art and culture appealed to them.

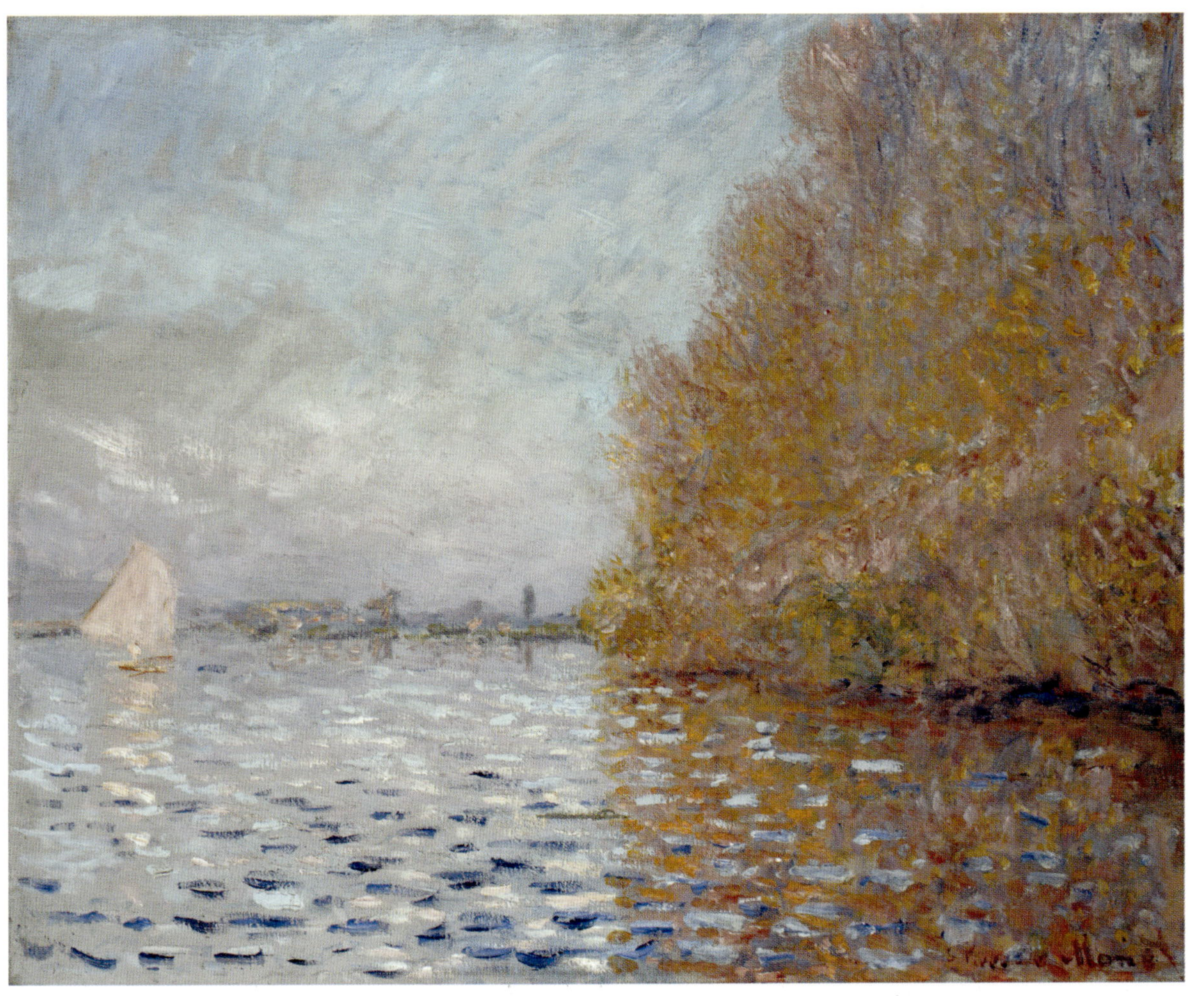

Claude Monet

Paris 1840–1926 Giverny

Argenteuil Basin with a Single Sailboat, 1874

Oil on canvas, 55 x 65 cm
Bequeathed, Edward Martyn, 1924
NGI.852

Monet lived in Argenteuil on the outskirts of Paris from 1871–78. During this period he fitted out a boat as a floating studio and produced many views of the River Seine and its banks. He painted this picture in 1874, the year that the first Impressionist exhibition was held in Paris. Monet has used distinct broken brushstrokes and complementary colours to suggest light and movement. The shifting clouds, rippled water, orange leaves and gliding yacht further evoke a sense of transience. Most of the scene is composed of sky and reflections.

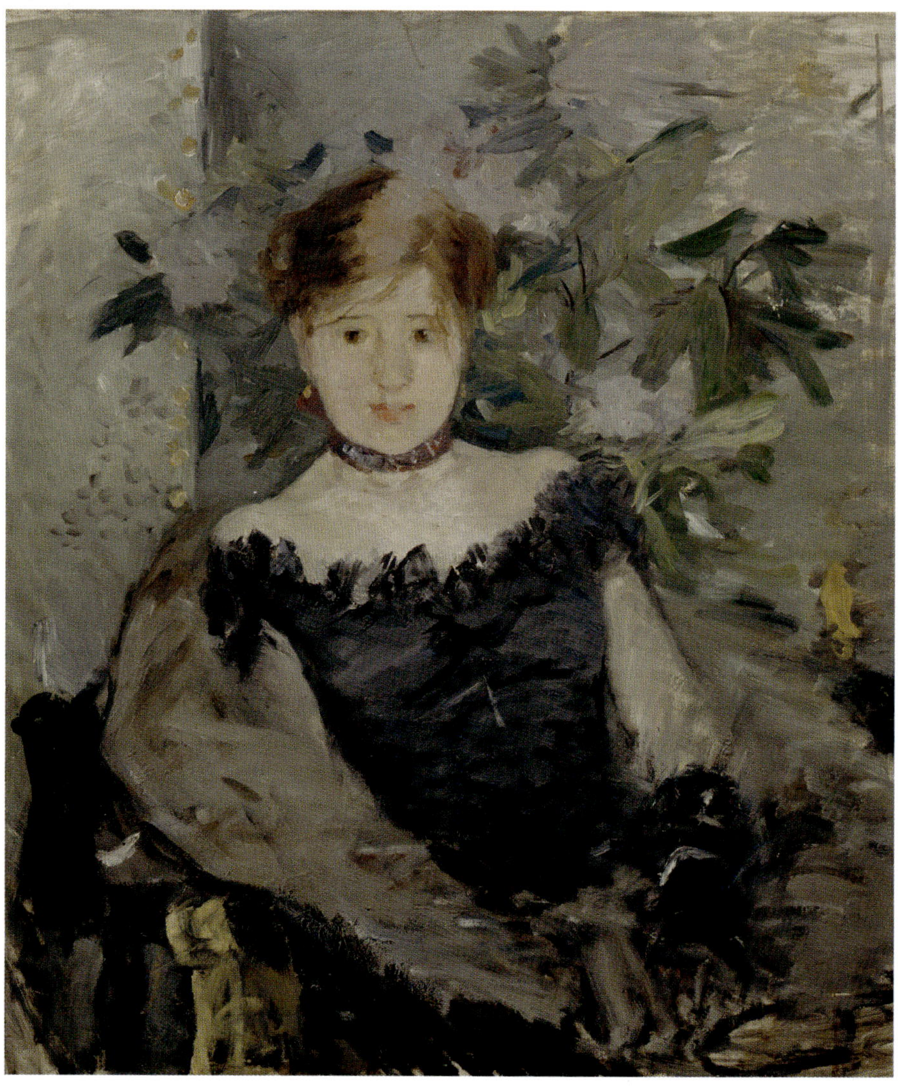

Berthe Morisot

Bourges 1841–1895 Paris

Le Corsage Noir, 1878

Oil on canvas, 73 x 65 cm
Purchased, 1936
NGI.984

Morisot was the only woman to exhibit at the first Impressionist exhibition of 1874 and at most of the group's subsequent shows. Although she did paint outdoor scenes, she is best known for her intimate domestic interiors. Here a young woman (posed by a professional model) is dressed for an evening at the theatre. The black gown to which the painting's title refers is accessorised with a stole, choker, earrings and gloves. Morisot uses broad brushstrokes for the woman's costume and the background foliage, while her treatment of the face and hair is more delicately handled.

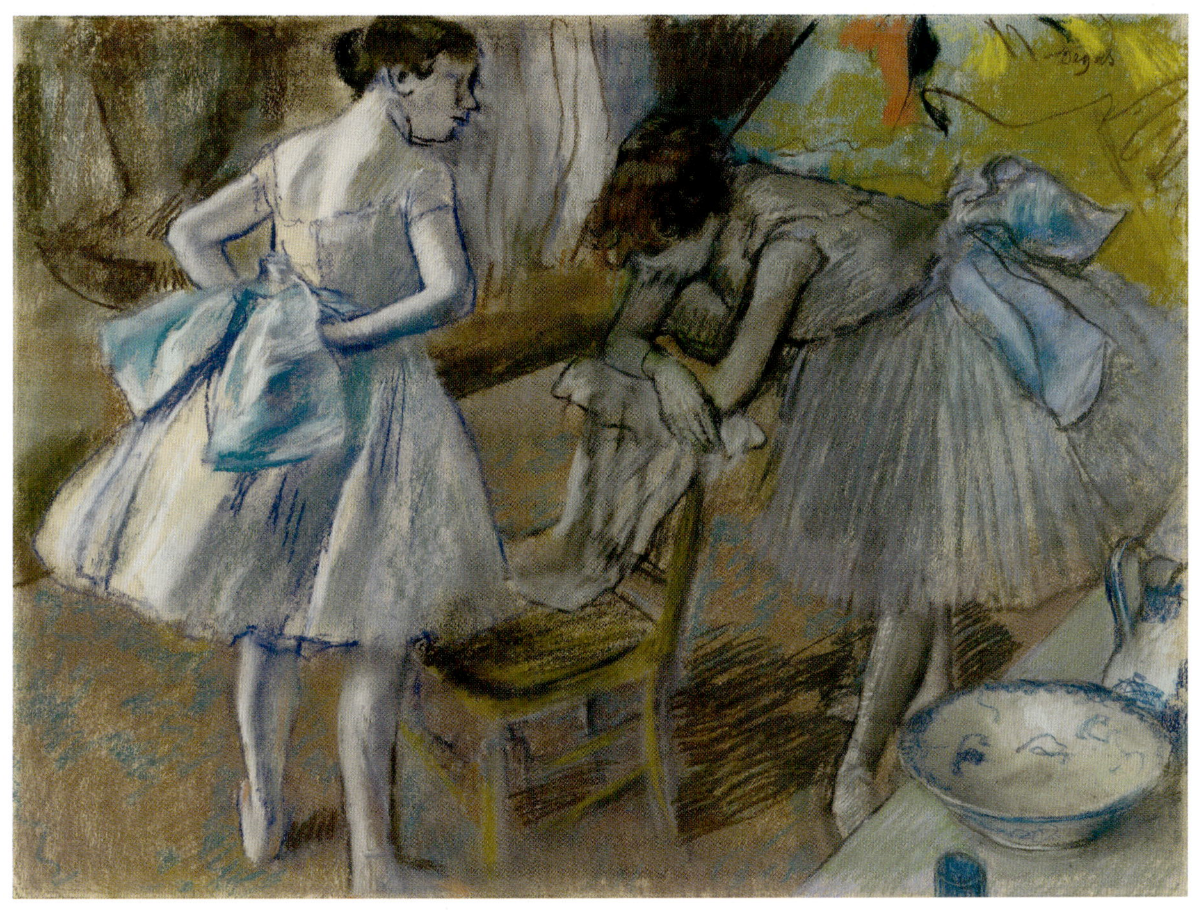

Edgar Degas

Paris, 1834–1917

Two Ballet Dancers in a Dressing Room, c.1880

Pastel on paper, 48.5 x 64 cm
Bequeathed, Edward Martyn, 1924
NGI.2740

Edgar Degas made countless studies of ballet dancers in rehearsal studios and backstage at the Paris Opéra, capturing their agile movements as they practised, stretched or simply waited. Degas was more interested in the realities of their routine work environment and rigorous training than their polished performances. From the 1880s he increasingly used pastel to depict their elegant tutus and contorted poses. These dancers appear unaware of the viewer. Glimpsed from an elevated viewpoint, one of them adjusts the blue sash of her costume while the other rests her forearms on a chair, a telling moment indicating her fatigue. The cropped nature of the composition contributes to the overall sense of immediacy of this image.

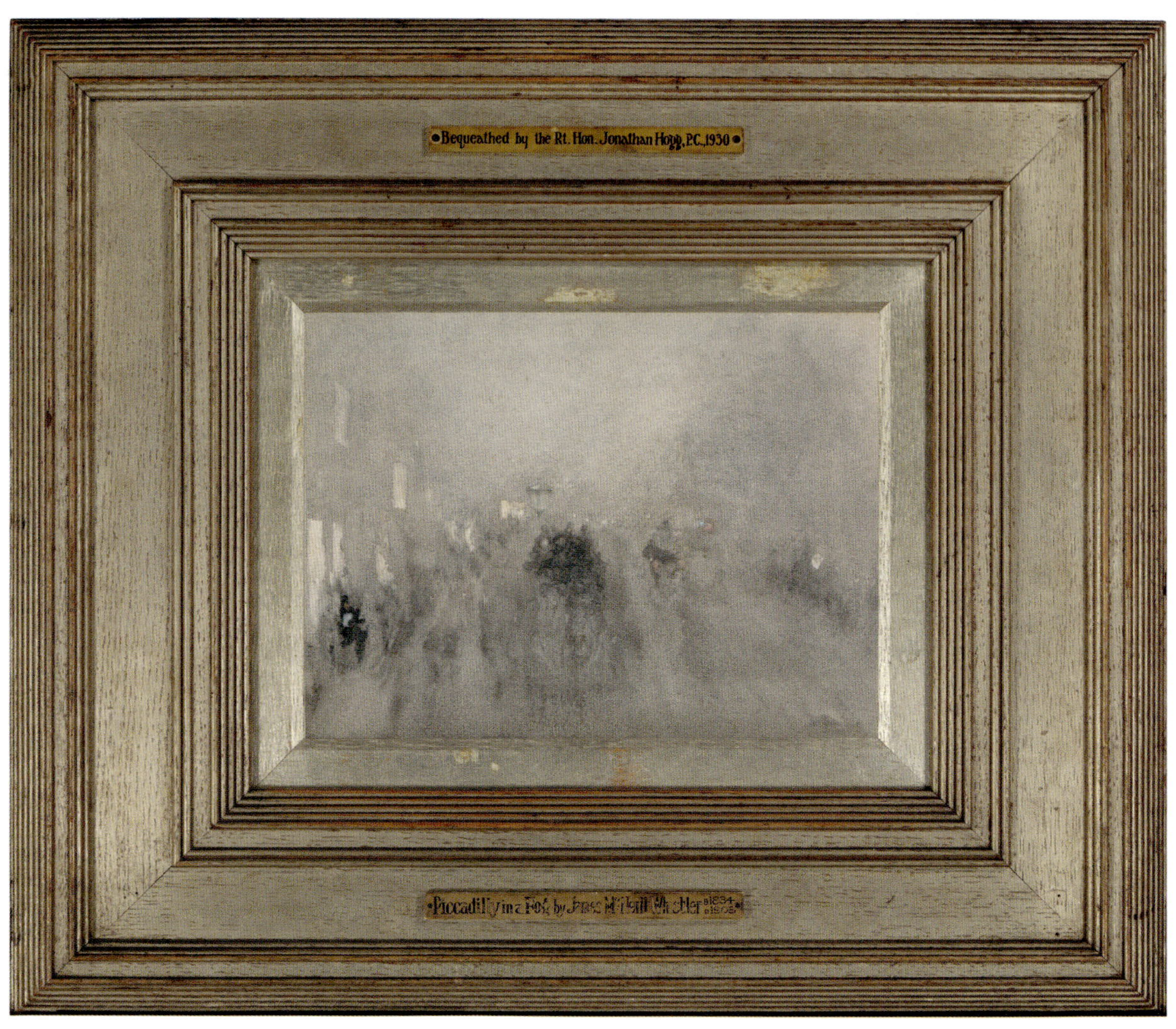

James Abbott McNeill Whistler

Lowell, Mass. 1834–1903 London

Nocturne in Grey and Gold – Piccadilly, 1881–1883

Watercolour on paper, 22.2 x 29.2 cm
Bequeathed, Right Honourable Jonathan Hogg, 1930
NGI.2915

Whistler wanted his paintings to be experienced as arrangements of colour and line rather than as representational images. This semi-abstract watercolour featured in the artist's 1884 exhibition *Notes – Harmonies – Nocturnes* at the Dowdeswell Galleries on London's New Bond Street. Whistler began experimenting with new ways of presenting and installing his art in the 1870s. In his exhibitions he controlled everything, from the design of the distinctive frame mouldings to the colour of the walls and the well-spaced layout of the pictures. The frame here is significant as it retains the original silver-gold gilding chosen by the artist himself.

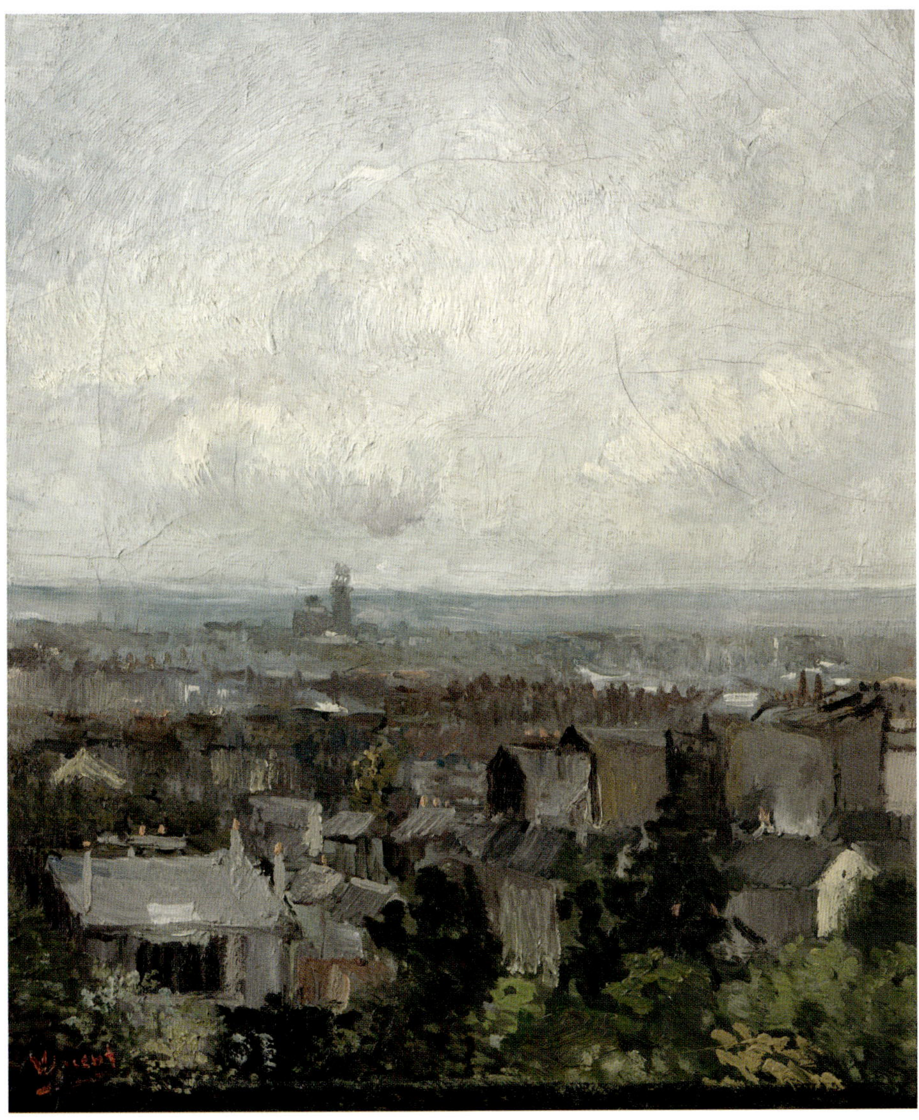

Vincent van Gogh

Zundert 1853–1890 Auvers-sur-Oise

Rooftops in Paris, 1886

Oil on canvas, 45.6 x 38.5 cm
Purchased, 2007
NGI.2007.2

Van Gogh arrived in Paris in 1886 and stayed with his brother Theo in his apartment on the Rue Lepic, near Montmartre. This is one of several panoramic views of the city that he made at this time. Painted from the Butte Montmartre, it shows the city extending south. During his first months in France, Van Gogh continued to paint in the dark tones typical of his early work in the Netherlands. Throughout his life, he was deeply fascinated with skies and cloud formations. Here, the low horizon line gives prominence to an expanse of grey sky, while vegetation and buildings are outlined in a dense *impasto* in the foreground.

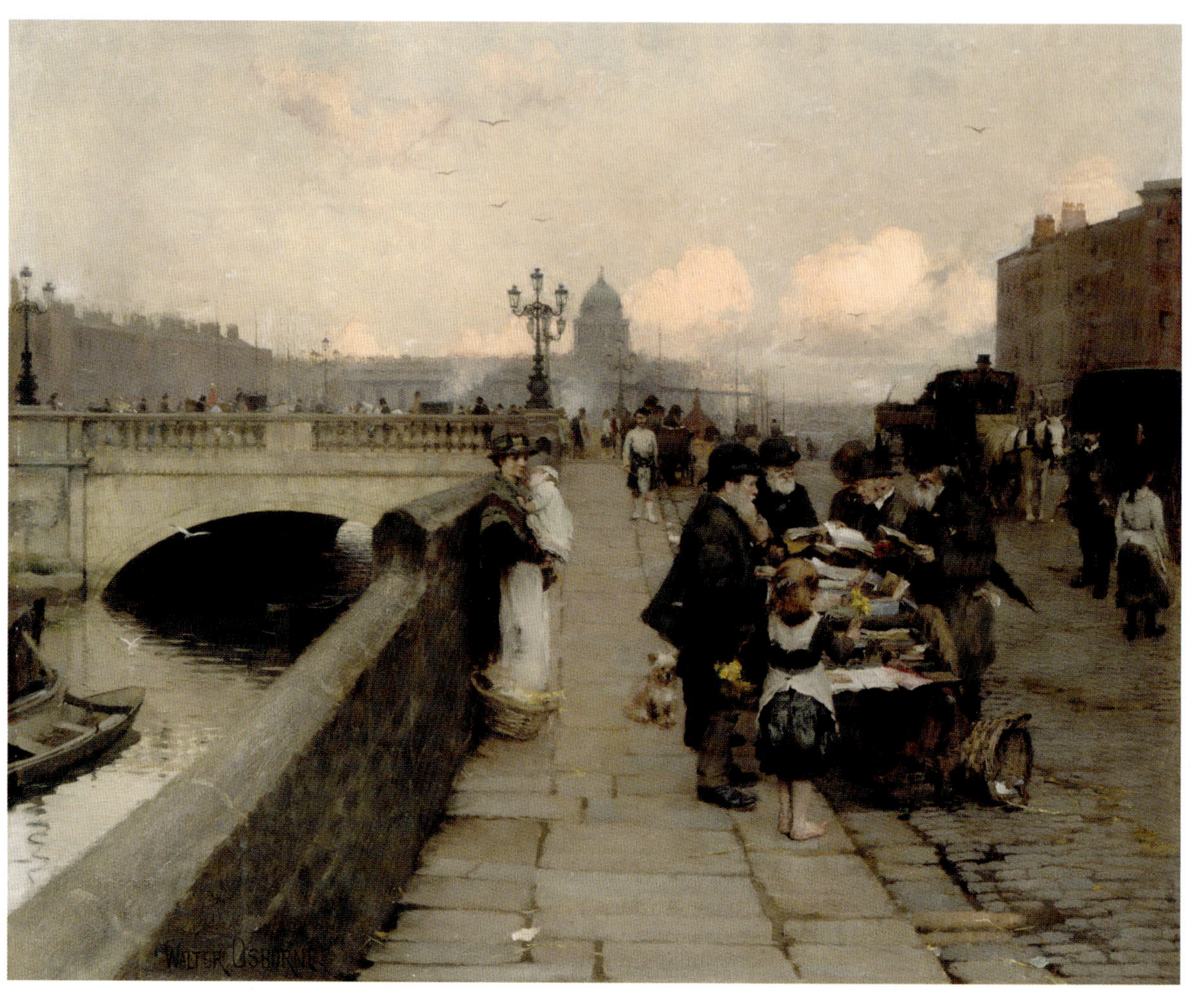

Walter Frederick Osborne
Dublin, 1859–1903
Dublin Streets: a Vendor of Books, 1889

Oil on canvas, 80 x 90 cm
Bequeathed, John Hamilton-Hunter, in memory of his father, Robert Hamilton-Hunter, 2004
NGI.4736

Aston Quay had been for generations a favourite location for street hawkers and stall holders. In Osborne's picture a mother with a baby appears to have dispatched an older child to charm gentlemen perusing books at the stall into buying daffodils. The little flower-girl's bare feet are an explicit reference to the hardships endured by Dublin's poor, while a barge and skiff serve as evidence of the Liffey's status as a working river. The painting features the remarkable view eastwards across the river towards James Gandon's Custom House that would soon be compromised by the building of the Loopline Bridge.

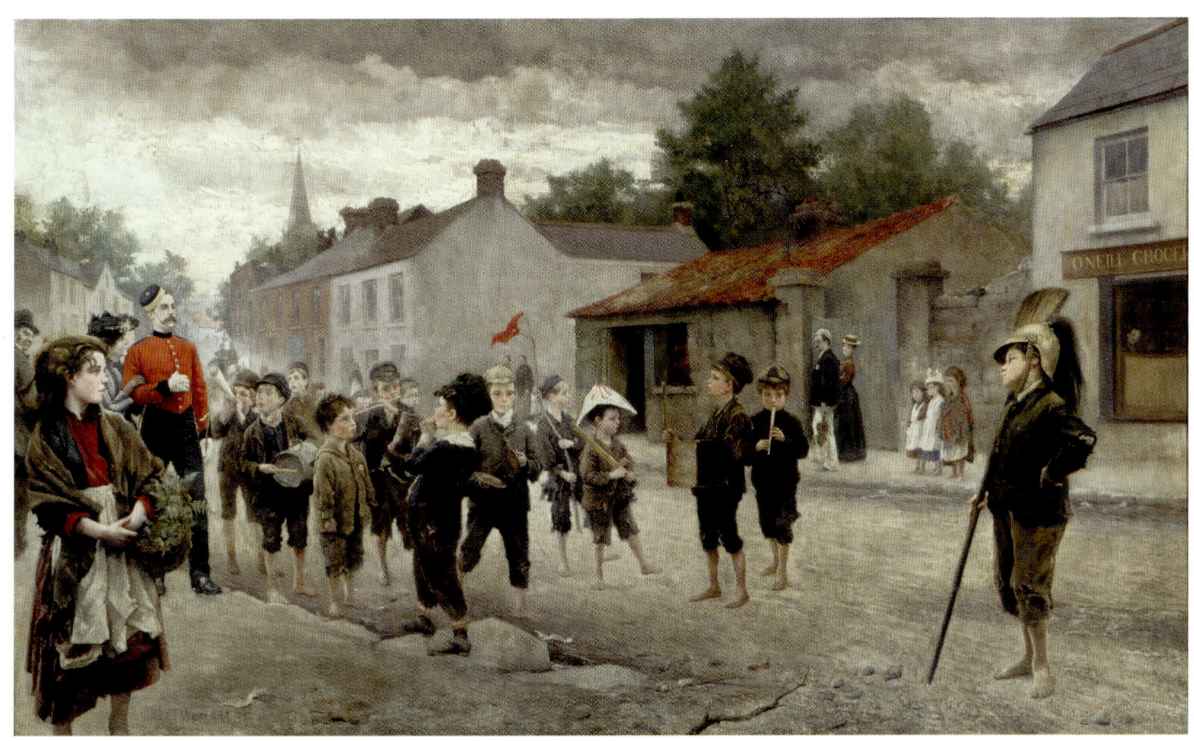

Richard Thomas Moynan

Dublin, 1856–1906

Military Manoeuvres, 1891

Oil on canvas, 148 x 240 cm
Purchased, 1982
NGI.4364

As they stroll along the main street in Leixlip, County Kildare, a trooper of the Fourth Royal Irish Dragoon Guards and his female companion find themselves shadowed by a group of ragged children pretending to be the members of a military band. Several try to attract the attention of the soldier but he remains resolutely aloof. The would-be drum major, waiting impatiently for his charges, wears the helmet of the regimental band, its black horse-hair plume clearly visible. Moynan painted many military subjects, including formal portraits, and was also admired for his skill in depicting children.

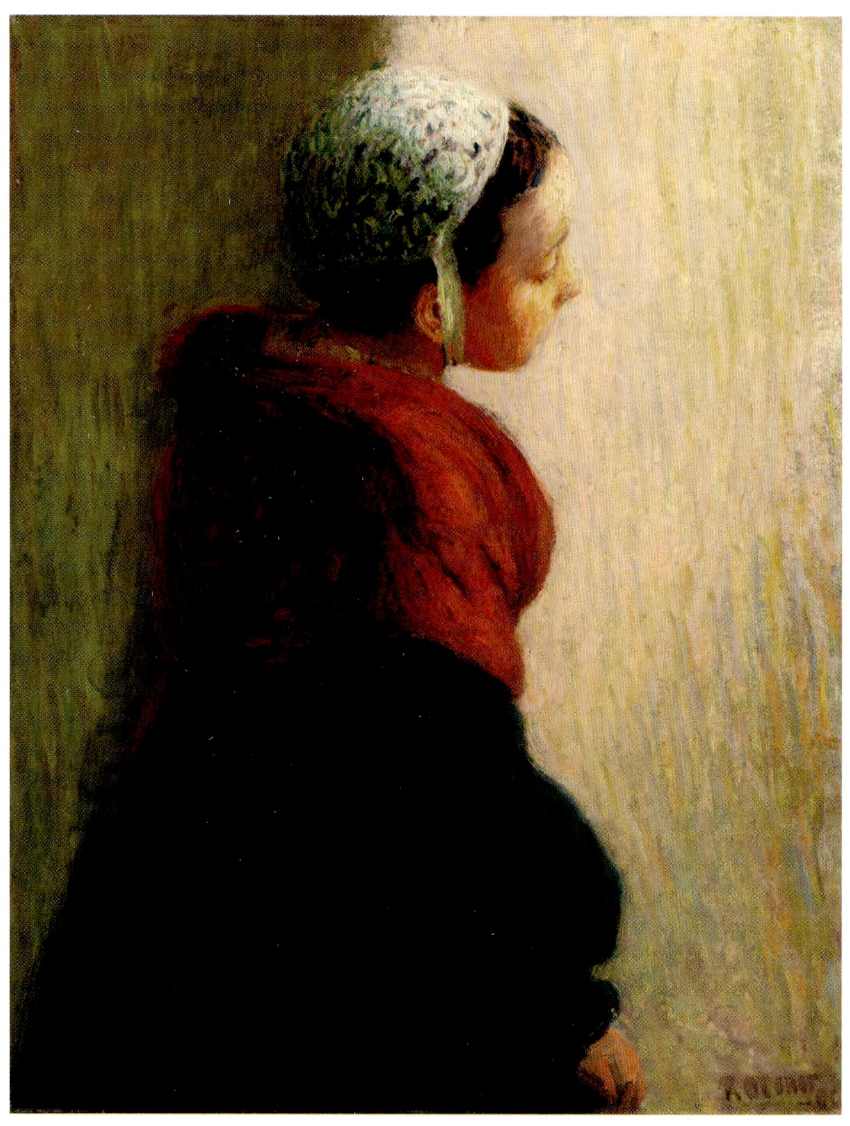

Roderic O'Conor

Milton (Milltown), County Roscommon 1860–1940 Neuil-sur-Layon

La Jeune Bretonne, c.1895

Oil on canvas, 65 x 50 cm
Purchased, 1975 (Shaw Fund)
NGI.4134

O'Conor painted several studies of young Breton women engaged in quiet activity or, as here, reverie. The subject is conventional and echoes the work of countless visitors to Brittany in the final decades of the nineteenth century. However, O'Conor records the local girl's traditional costume as much for its pictorial qualities as for its cultural significance. O'Conor's associates in Brittany included Gauguin and Serusier, and though their influence was apparent in the Irishman's increasingly expressive technique and use of vibrant colour, O'Conor's style remained distinctively his own. The deliberate juxtaposition of opposing colours would become typical of the artist's work.

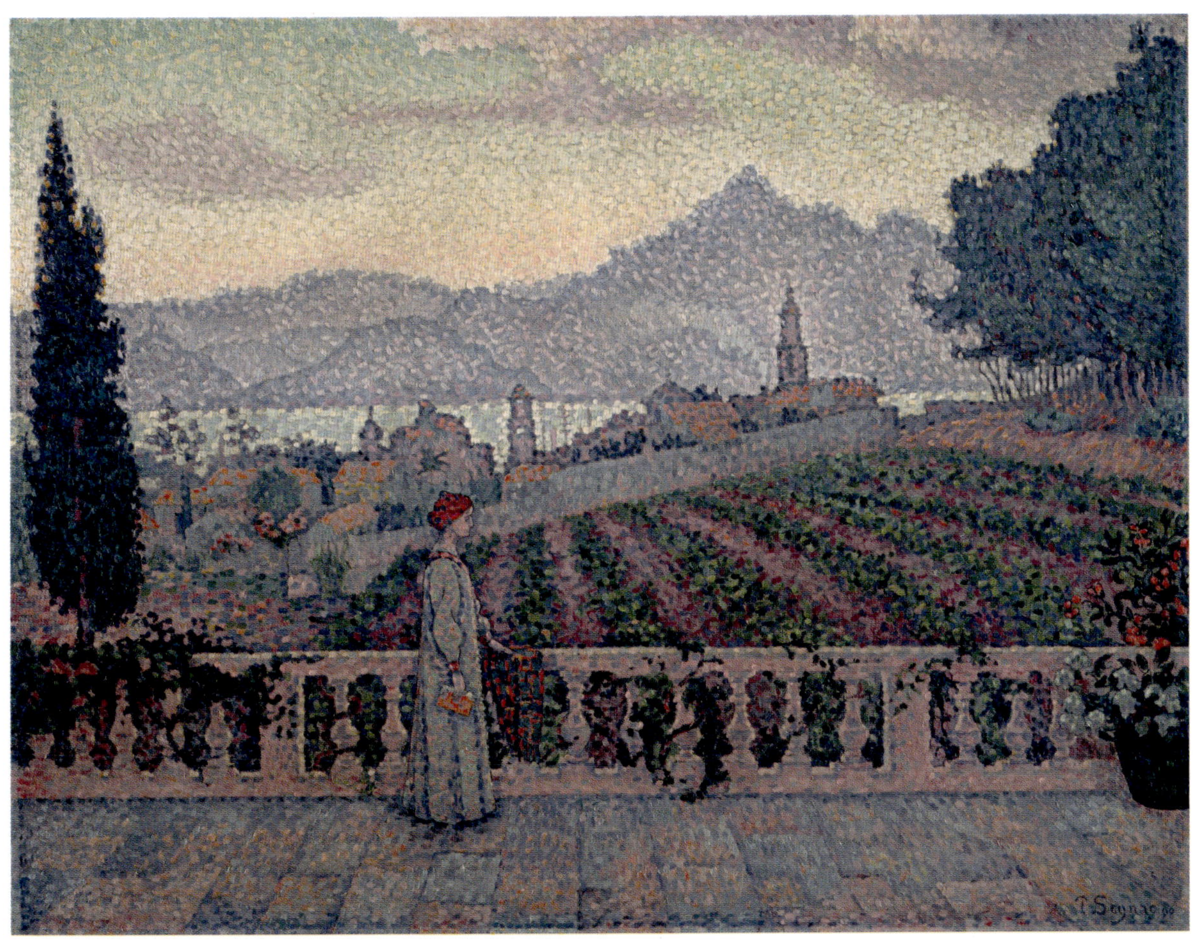

Paul Signac

Paris, 1863–1935

The Terrace, Saint-Tropez, 1898

Oil on canvas, 72.5 x 91.5 cm
Purchased, 1982 (Shaw Fund)
NGI.4361

With Georges Seurat, Signac developed a style of painting known as Pointillism, a technique that involved applying dots of pure colour directly onto canvas, with the intention that they would merge in the eyes and mind of the observer. This scene is set on the terrace of Signac's villa *La Hune* in Saint-Tropez. The artist's wife Berthe modelled for the female figure. At the end of the nineteenth century Signac developed an interest in Italian frescoes of the Quattrocento, something that is reflected in the Italianate landscape, vibrant colouring and matt finish of this work.

1900–present

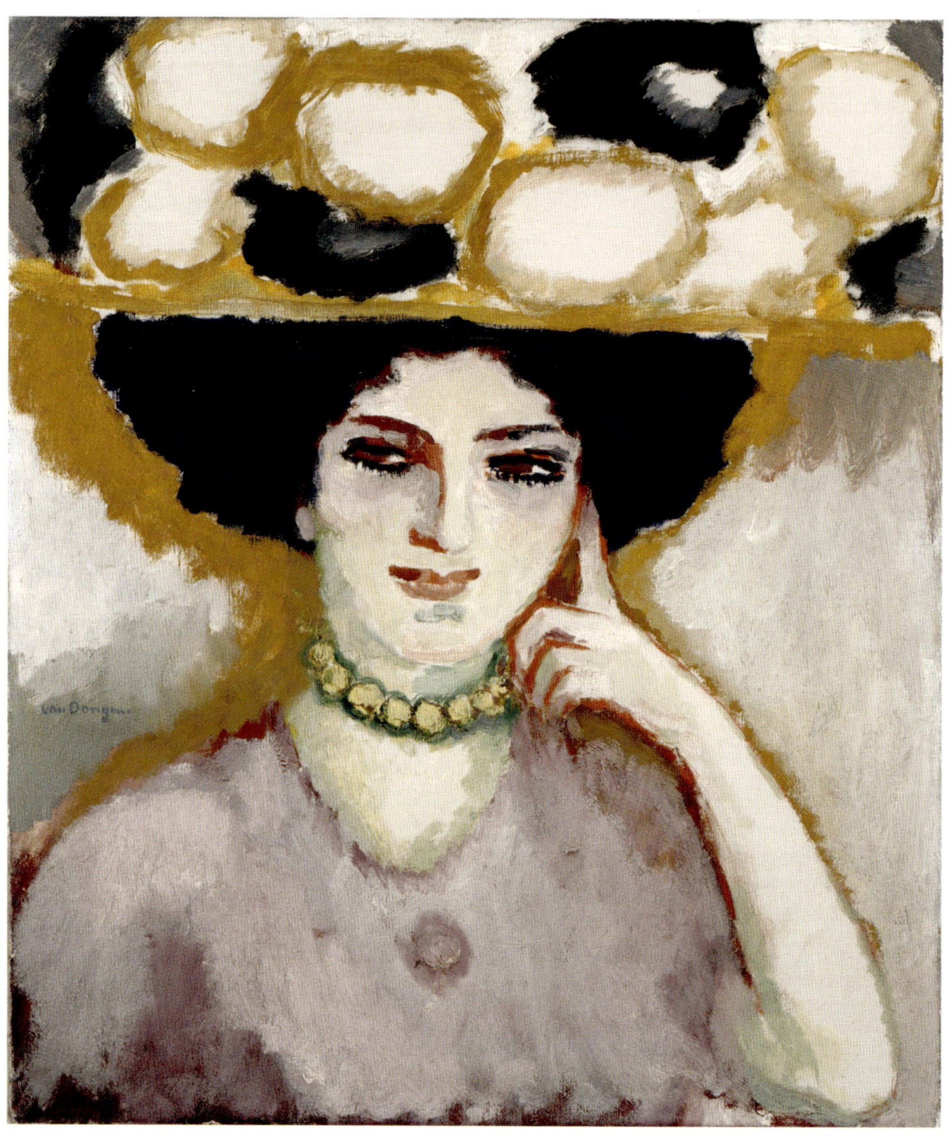

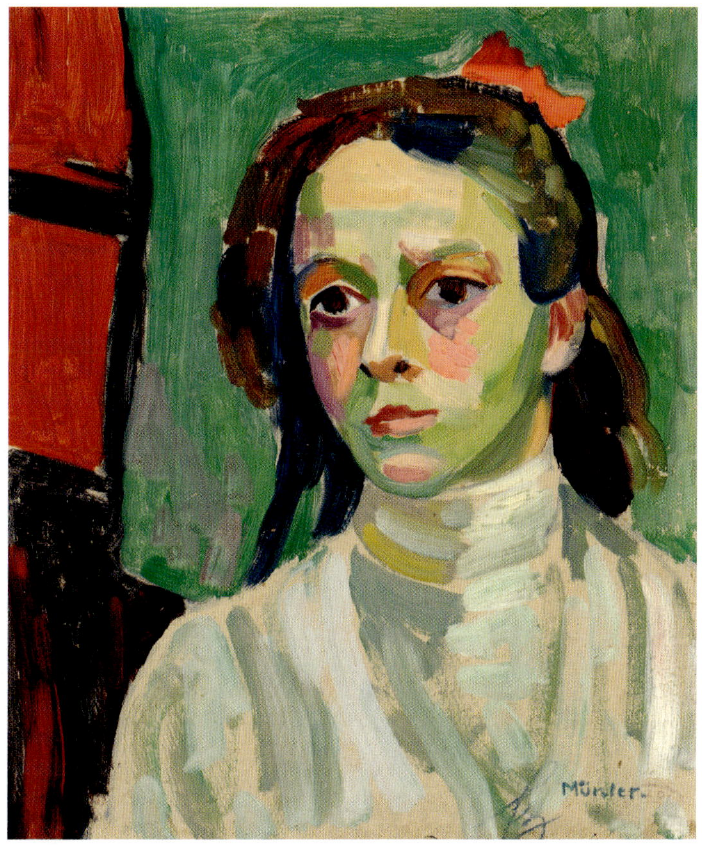

◄ **Kees van Dongen**

Delfshaven 1877–1968 Monaco

Stella in a Flowered Hat, c.1907

Oil on canvas, 65 x 54 cm
Purchased, 1981 (Shaw Fund)
NGI.4355

The Dutch artist Kees van Dongen captured the sensual cabaret and night-club performers of Paris with stark honesty. This woman's hand gesture suggests pensiveness, while her sideways glance is seductive. The violent colours used are decorative and expressive rather than naturalistic: green for the shadows on Stella's throat, purple for her face and red for her eyes. Van Dongen spent most of his career in France, where he was associated with Henri Matisse and the 'Fauves', a term meaning 'savages' or 'wild beasts', used in reference to this group of artists' use of vivid and intense colour.

▲ **Gabriele Münter**

Berlin 1877–1962 Murnau

Girl with a Red Ribbon, 1908

Oil on board, 40.7 x 32.8 cm
Purchased, 2006
NGI.2006.12

Gabriele Münter was a leading German Expressionist. In 1908, with her partner, Wassily Kandinsky, she settled in the village of Murnau in the lake district of southern Bavaria. Dated 1908, this vibrant painting is from a time when Münter claimed her work advanced greatly. The girl, perhaps a local villager, wears a high-collared white blouse and a red ribbon in her hair. The green, red, purple and pink hues in her face reveal the influence of Vincent van Gogh and Henri Matisse on the artist. Also at play are German folk art and Bavarian glass-painting, the latter evident in the flat background colours separated by heavy, dark lines.

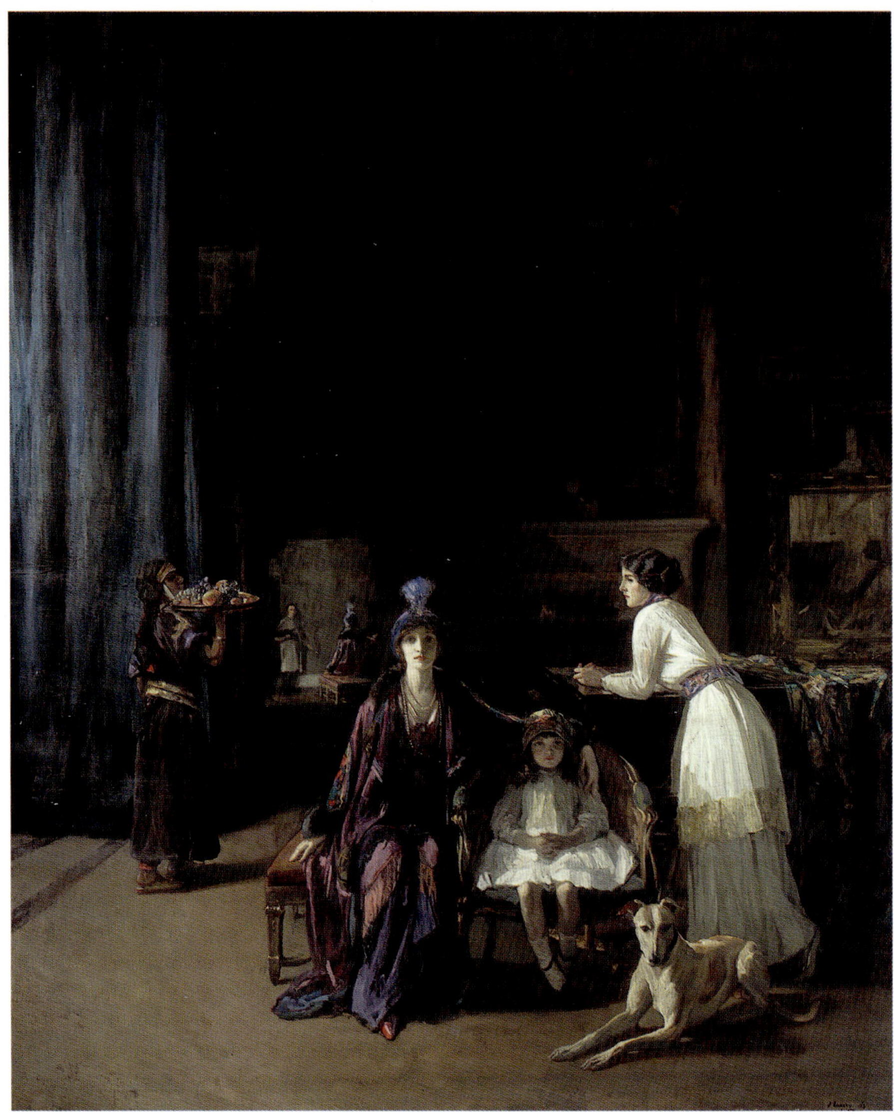

John Lavery

Belfast 1856–1941 Kilkenny

The Artist's Studio: Lady Hazel Lavery with her Daughter Alice and Stepdaughter Eileen, 1910–1913

Oil on canvas, 344 x 274 cm
Purchased, 1959
NGI.1644

Set in the artist's lofty workroom in London, this huge picture features Lavery's wife Hazel, her daughter Alice from her first marriage and the artist's daughter Eileen by his first wife. To the left is the family's Moroccan maid Aïda, whose presence alludes to the artist's long-standing relationship with North Africa. Lavery based both the painting's overall composition and some prominent details on Velázquez's *Las Meninas*, placing the family greyhound, for example, in the same spot as that occupied by a dog in the seventeenth-century painting and including his own reflection, holding his palette and brush, in the background.

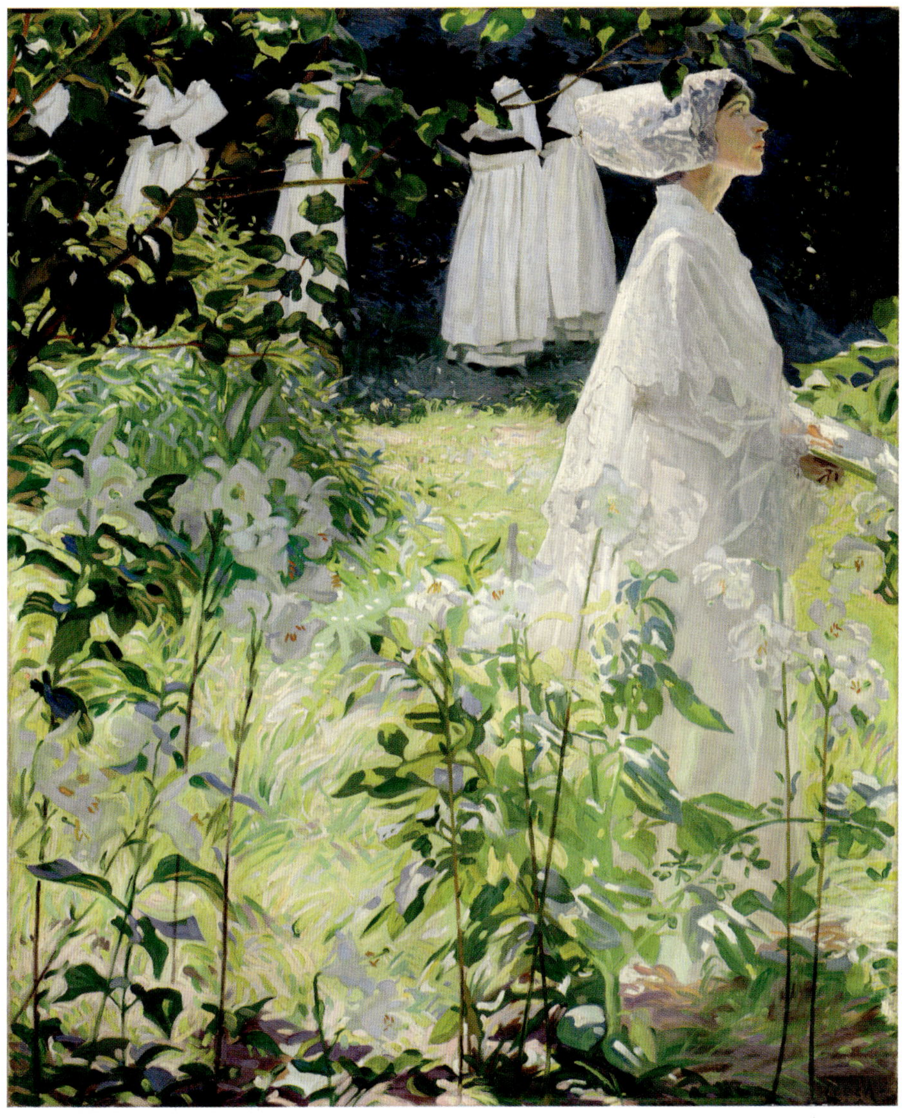

William John Leech

Dublin 1881–1968 Guildford

A Convent Garden, Brittany, c.1913

Oil on canvas, 132 x 106 cm
Presented, Mrs M. Botterell, 1952
NGI.1245

In this picture, Leech's first wife Elizabeth, posing as a novice of the Soeurs du Saint-Esprit, looks up from her prayer book as nuns from the same order process in the background. Elizabeth wears the Breton bridal costume traditionally donned by novices on the day they took their final vows. The setting is the walled garden of the nuns' hospital and convent in Concarneau, in which Leech had convalesced in 1904. The painting reflects an interest in the religious devotion of the Breton community that Leech shared with many visiting artists, but also the artist's love of sunlight and pattern.

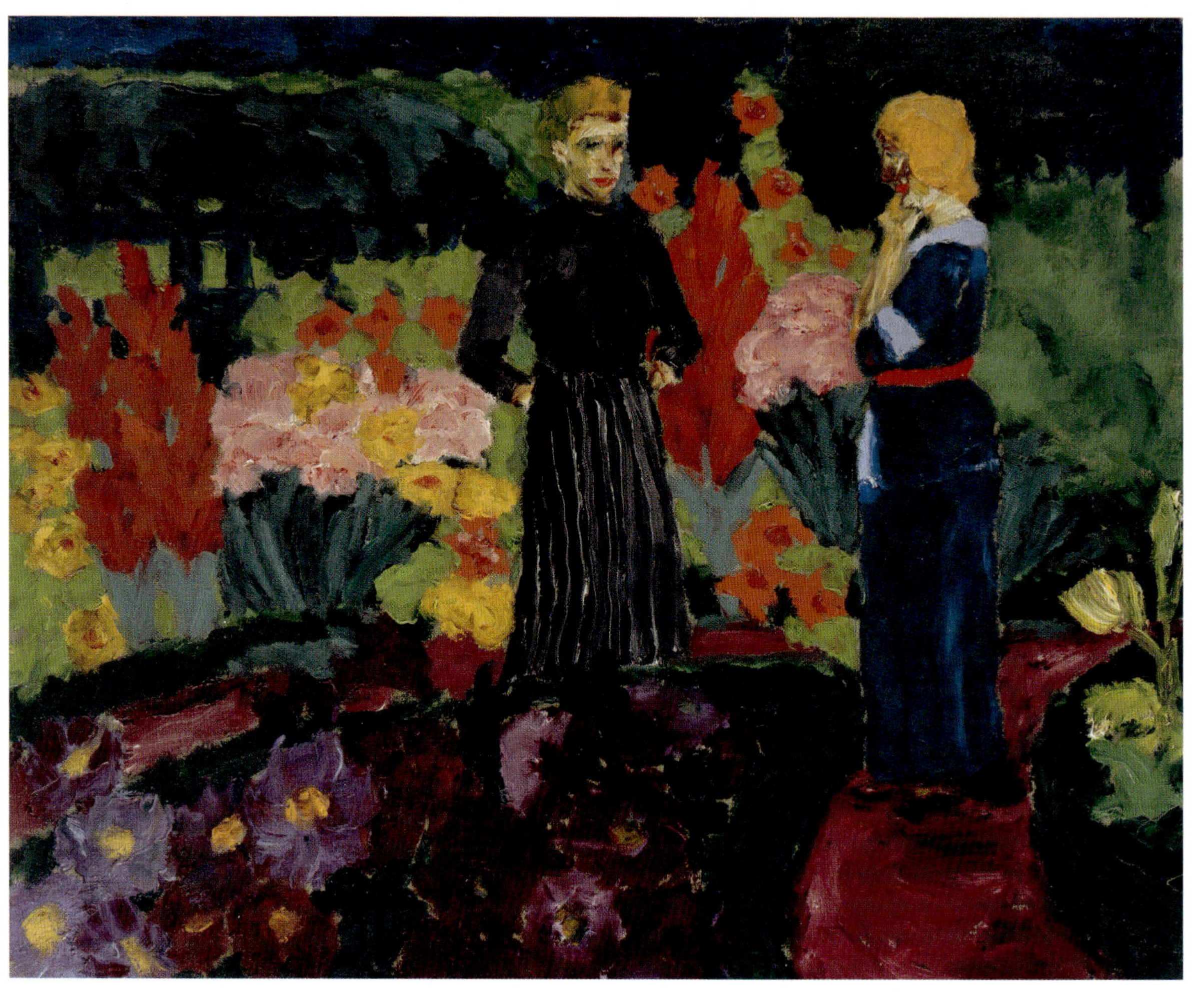

Emil Nolde

Nolde, Schleswig-Holstein 1867–1956
Seebüll, Schleswig-Holstein

Two Women in a Garden, 1915

Oil on canvas, 73 x 88 cm
Purchased, 1984 (Shaw Fund)
NGI.4490

Emil Nolde was one of the principal exponents of German Expressionism. He was a member of the Dresden-based Die Brücke group from 1906–07. With the onset of the First World War Nolde turned away from urban subject matter, preferring instead to concentrate on nature and rural contexts. He painted this vibrant picture at his cottage on the island of Alsen. Executed in a dense *impasto*, it depicts two women conversing among colourful flowers. The model for the woman in profile was the artist's wife Ada.

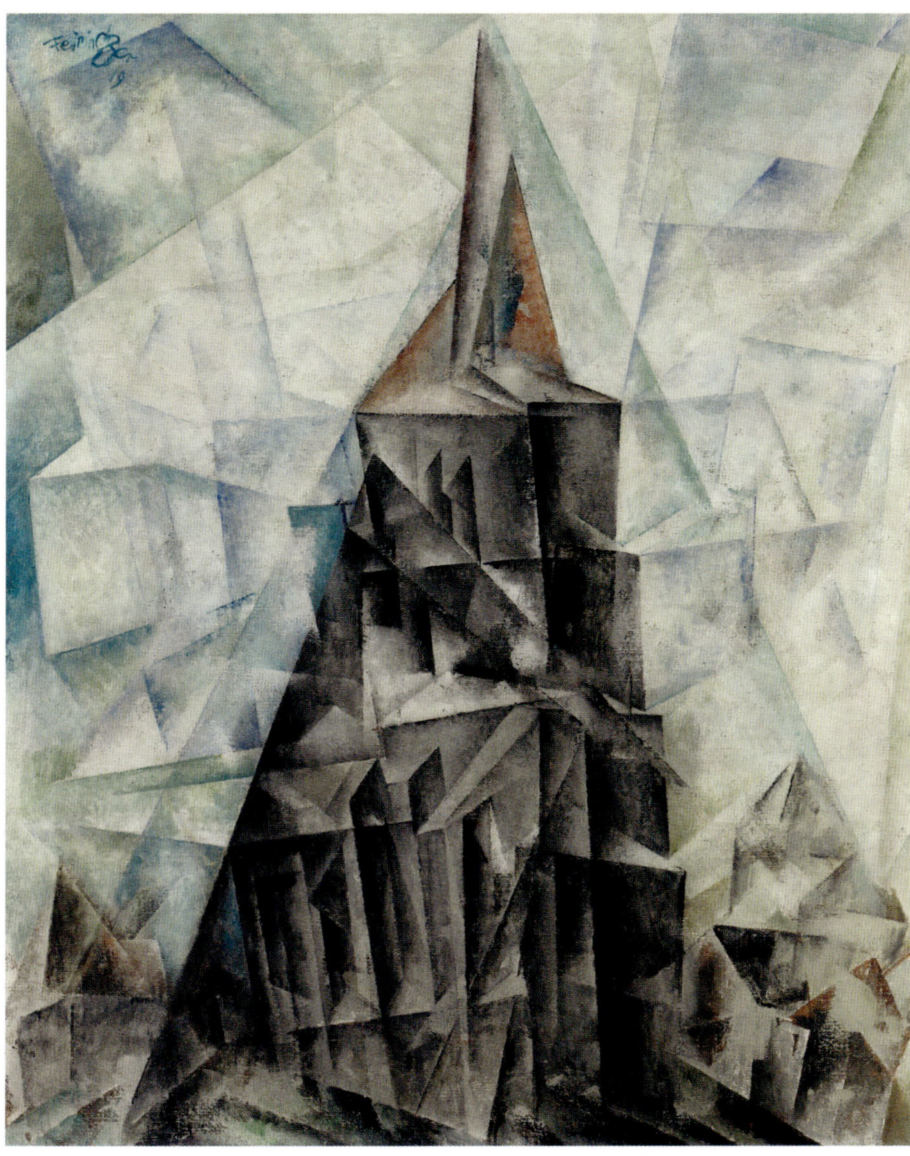

Lyonel Feininger

New York, 1871–1956

Umpferstedt III, 1919

Oil on canvas, 101 x 80 cm
Purchased, 2008
NGI.2008.91

Feininger was an American artist who worked in Germany for several decades before returning to the United States in 1937. This work is one of three paintings that he made inspired by the picturesque village of Umpferstedt in the Weimar region. Its facetted forms and restrained dynamism reveal Feininger's interest in Orphic Cubism. Feininger became head of the graphic workshop of the newly founded Bauhaus in 1919. His woodcut print *Cathedral of Socialism* (1919), designed as the first cover of the Bauhaus manifesto, is very similar in composition to this post-war depiction of Umpferstedt.

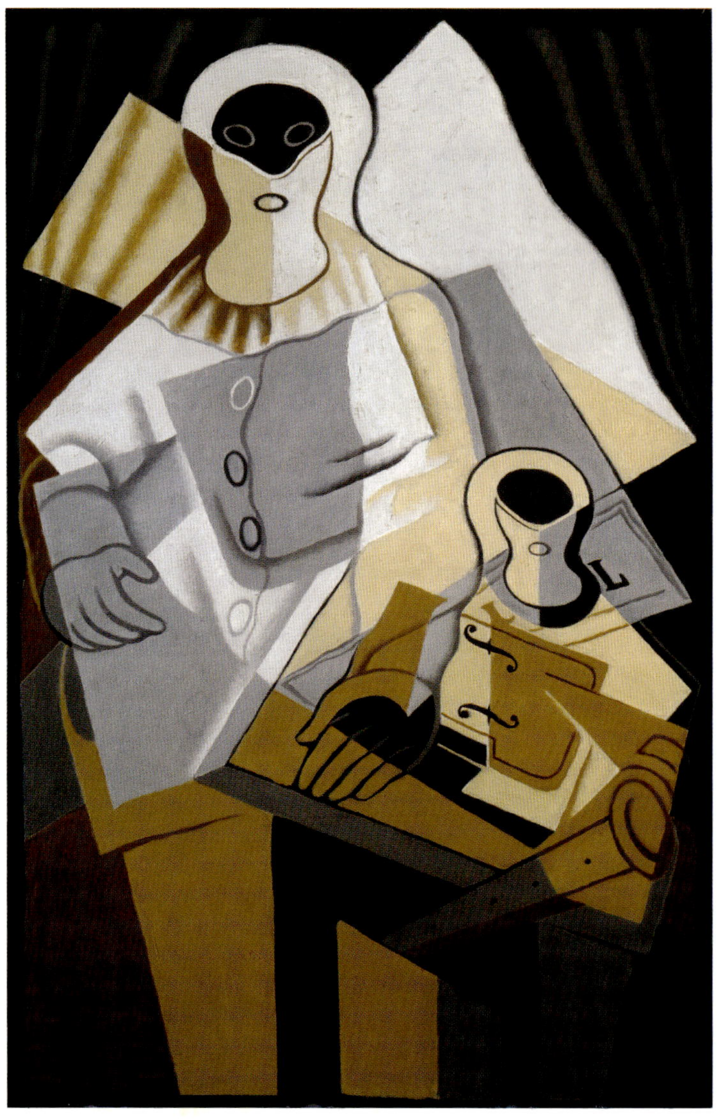

Juan Gris

Madrid 1887–1927 Paris

Pierrot, 1921

Oil on canvas, 115 x 73 cm
Bequeathed, Máire MacNeill Sweeney, 1987
NGI.4521

Having trained in his native Madrid, Gris moved to Paris in 1906, where he came in contact with the Cubist painters Pablo Picasso and Georges Braque, who influenced his work. In 1921 Gris began designing sets and costumes for Diaghilev's *Ballets Russes* and became fascinated with the masks and costumes of the *Commedia dell'Arte*. He was interested in the melancholic aspects of Pierrot's character and here gives him a tragic, masked face. The clown is part of a pattern of interlocking pieces, including a goblet, a violin, a clarinet, a newspaper and a table, all of which have been reduced to a series of overlapping planes.

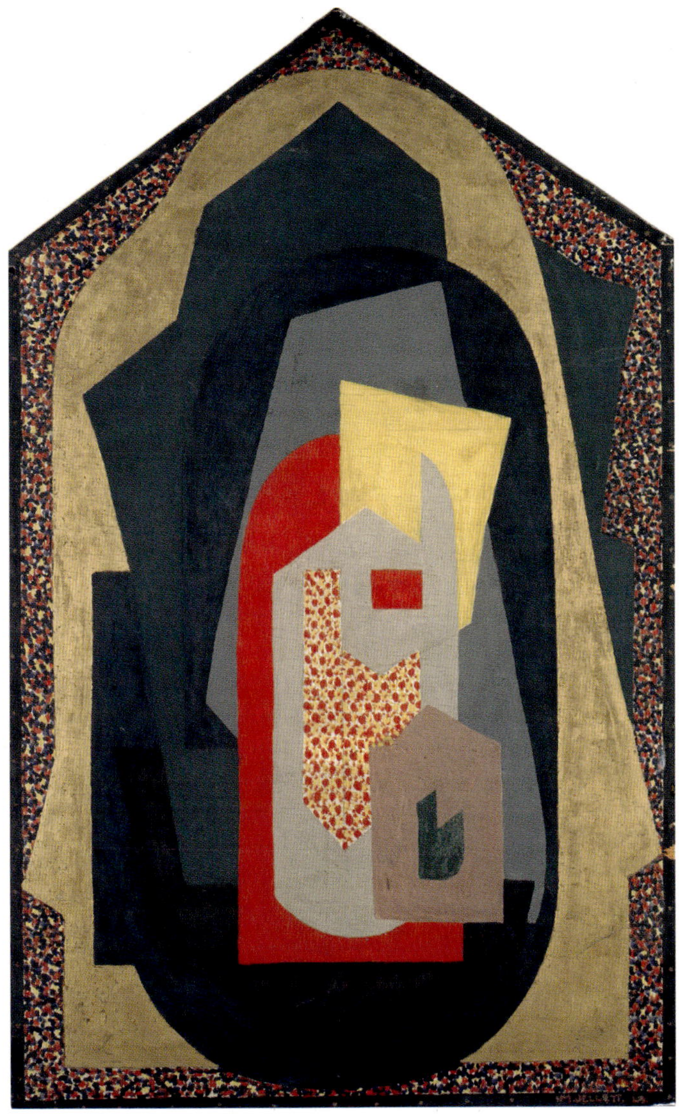

Mainie Jellett

Dublin, 1897–1944

Decoration, 1923

Tempera on wood panel, 89 x 53 cm
Bequeathed, Evie Hone, 1955
NGI.1326

Jellett trained in Dublin and London before moving on in 1920 to Paris. There, with Evie Hone, she studied under André Lhote, an advocate of Cézanne's analytical approach to painting, and Albert Gleizes, an established Cubist artist. Inspired by their work, Jellett began to analyse rhythm, colour and form in her own work, while also drawing on long-standing pictorial traditions. Though essentially abstract, the format, colour range and media of this work strongly recall religious icons depicting the Madonna and Child. When shown with a similarly abstract painting at the Society of Dublin Painters group show in 1923, *Decoration* caused a furore.

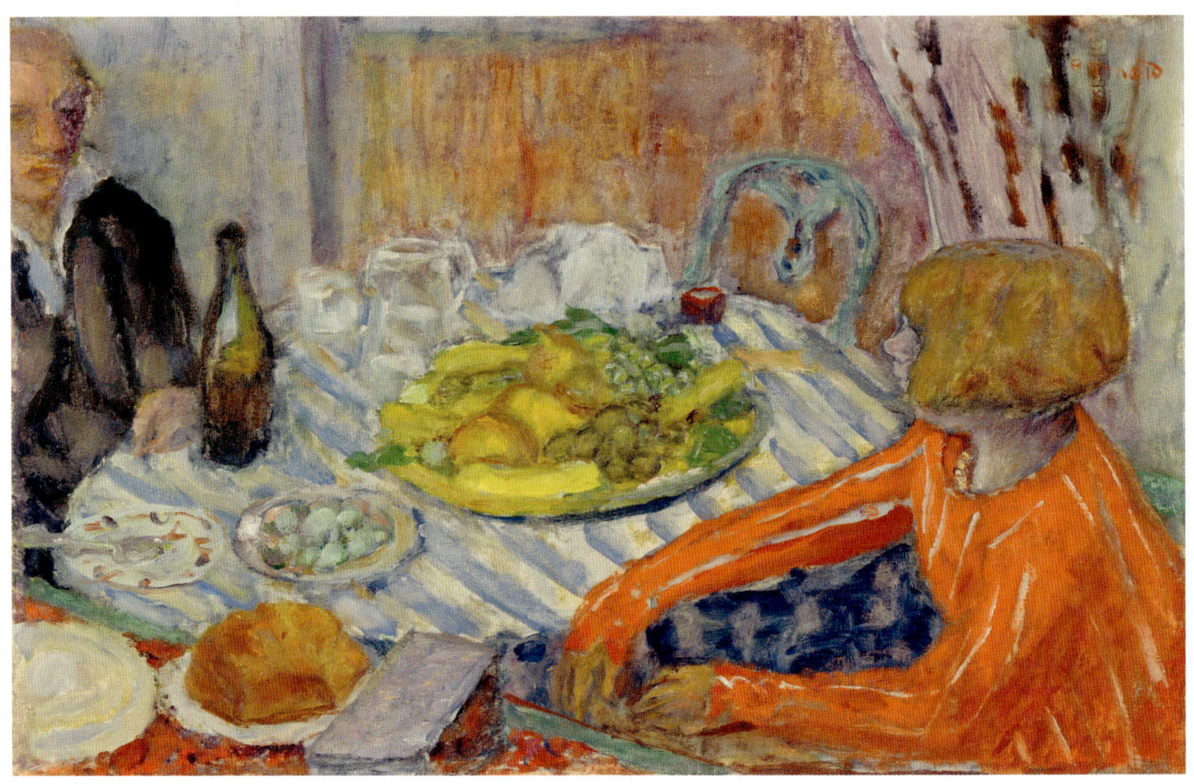

Pierre Bonnard

Fontenay-aux-Roses 1867–1947 Le Cannet

Le Déjeuner, 1923

Oil on canvas, 41.3 x 62.2 cm
Purchased, 2006
NGI.2006.23

Le Déjeuner is set in the dining room of the artist's country house *Ma Roulotte* (My Caravan), near Giverny. Bonnard painted many informal interiors there, which were typical of the style and subject matter of the *Intimiste* painters. A man, probably the artist, sits opposite Bonnard's long-time companion Marthe. The remains of their lunch appear to float on a tilted table-top, its perspective distorted. A snapshot effect is created by the cropping of the figures and objects at the edges of the composition. Influenced by Japanese prints, Bonnard contrasts flat, striped patterns, as in Marthe's red shirt and the blue-and-white tablecloth.

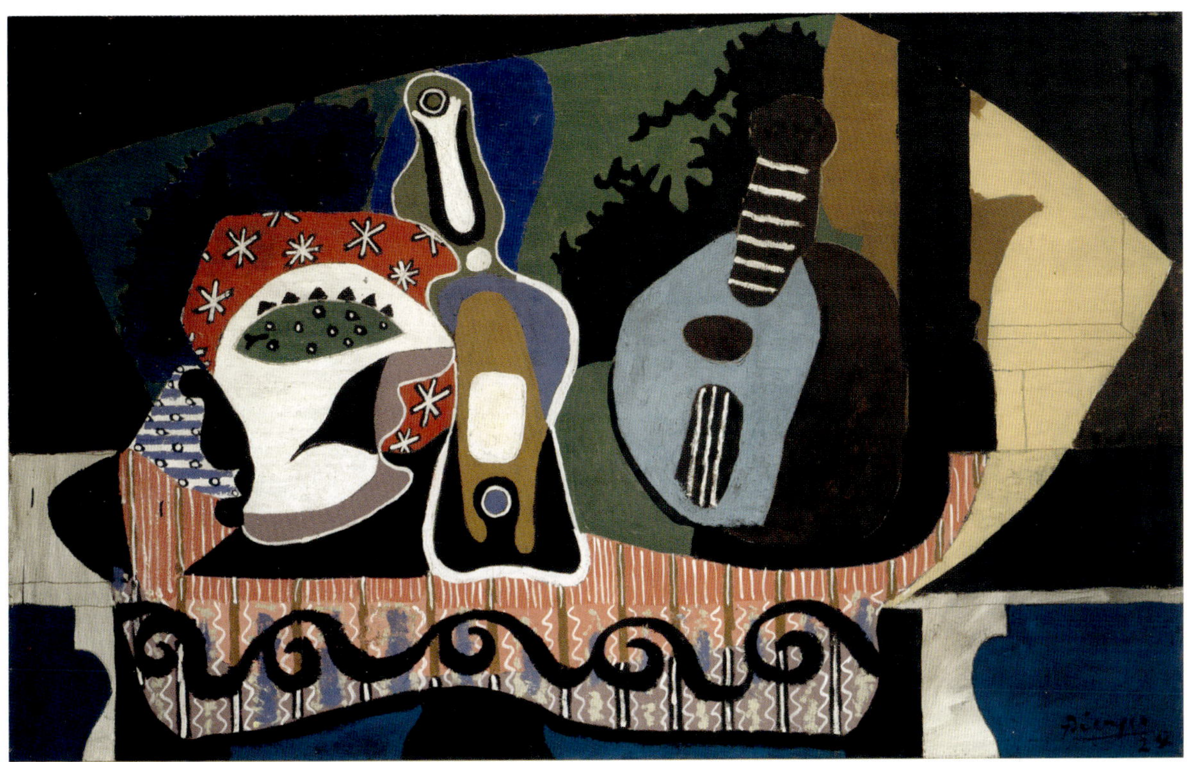

Pablo Picasso

Malaga 1881–1973 Mougins

Still Life with a Mandolin, 1924

Oil on canvas, 101 x 158 cm
Bequeathed, Máire MacNeill Sweeney, 1987
NGI.4522

In Paris, Picasso, along with the French artist Georges Braque, invented Cubism. This modern movement aimed to express the structure of an object by depicting it as a series of planes, seen from a number of different viewpoints simultaneously. Picasso spent the summer of 1924 in Juan-les-Pins, on the Mediterranean, creating still-life paintings in a bold, Cubist style. The distorted, organic shapes in this picture denote a fruit dish, a bottle and a mandolin. These objects are arranged on a table covered with patterned fabric, behind which bushes and cacti are silhouetted. The decorative, vibrant colours reveal the influence of Henri Matisse, whose work Picasso greatly admired.

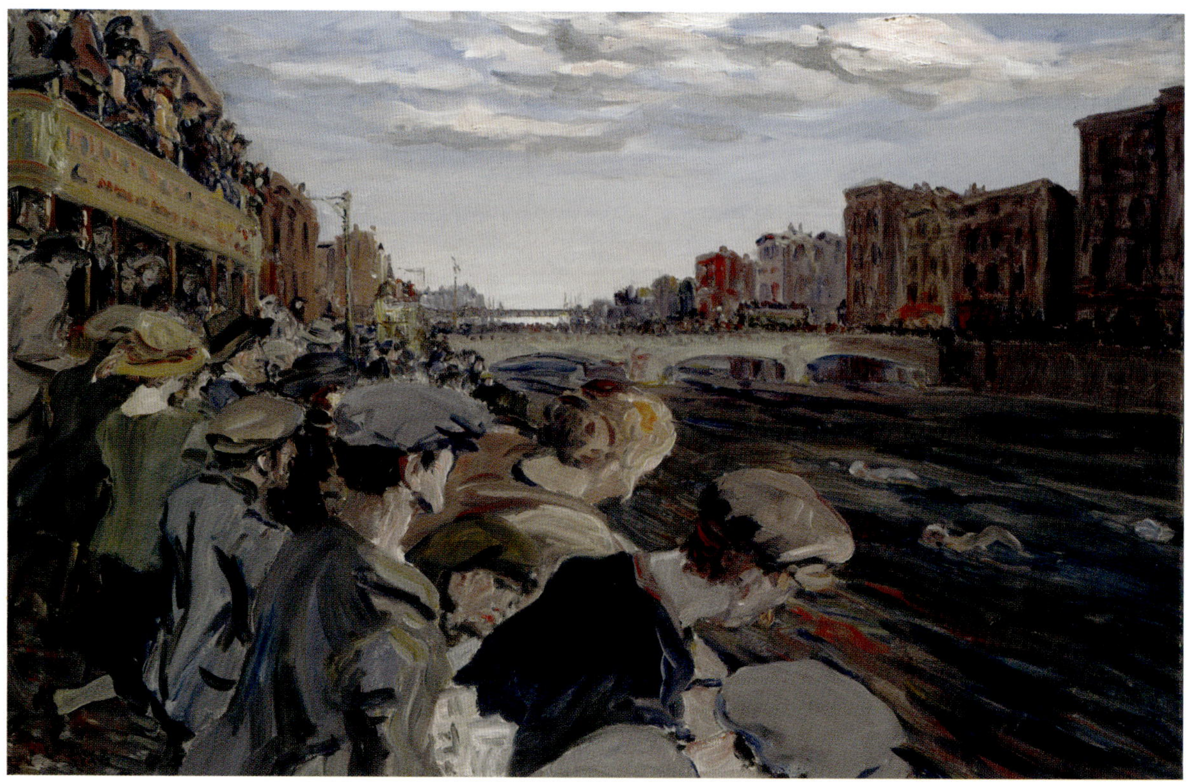

▲ **Jack B. Yeats**

London 1871–1957 Dublin

The Liffey Swim, 1923

Oil on canvas, 61 x 91 cm
Presented, Trustees of the Haverty Trust, 1931
NGI.941

In this painting, Yeats captures the atmosphere and thrill of an event that has been part of Dublin's annual sporting calendar since 1920. His depiction of the occasion also represents a return to the sporting themes that had inspired much of his early work. He invites his audience to engage with the event by placing them among the spectators, who lean forward to catch a glimpse of the swimmers as they surge towards the finish line. The painting marked Yeats's growing interest in Expressionism and his adoption of fluid brushwork and a charged palette.

▶ **William Orpen**

Dublin 1878–1931 London

Portrait of John Count McCormack (1884–1945), Tenor, 1923

Oil on canvas, 104 x 86.4 cm
Purchased, 2009
NGI.2009.11

Orpen manages to represent McCormack's imposing stature without making this the dominant characteristic of the portrait. Though the sitter's relaxed pose and tennis attire seem rather incongruous with the discipline at which he excelled, they are consistent with numerous portrayals of classical singers of the period. Indeed, the presentation of McCormack in casual attire is apposite, as the painting coincided with McCormack's decision to retire from opera and concentrate on more relaxed concert performances. The portrait demonstrates Orpen's renowned facility in capturing physical likeness and character, his technical virtuosity and innovative use of colour.

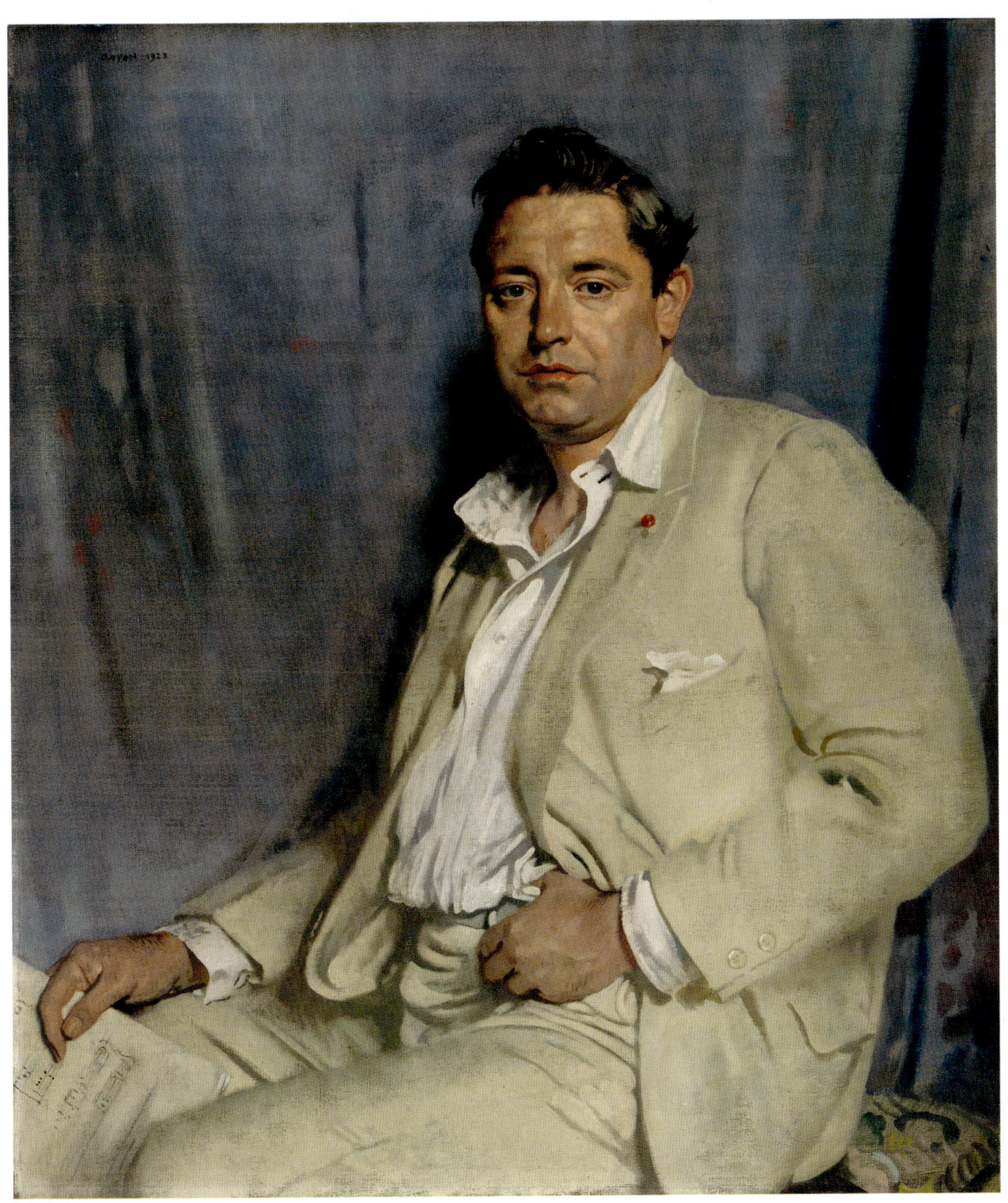

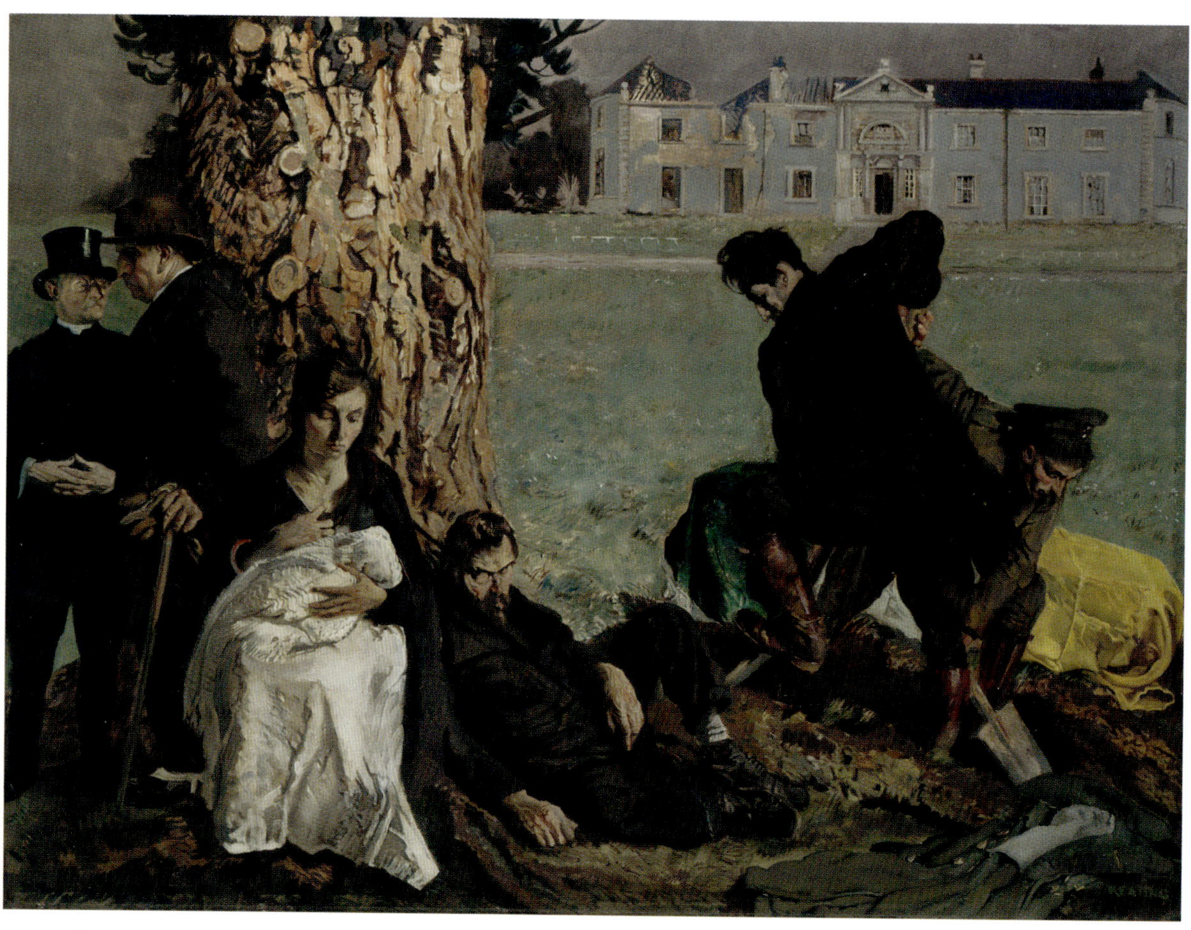

Seán Keating

Limerick 1889–1977 Dublin

An Allegory, 1924

Oil on canvas, 102 x 130 cm
Presented, Friends of the National Collections of Ireland, 1952
NGI.1236

Painted in the wake of the Irish Civil War, *An Allegory* is one of several works in which Keating addressed social and political matters affecting contemporary Ireland. In the painting, the artist expresses dismay at the destructive character of the conflict and communicates his suspicion of the clerical, political and business elite. As well as registering the human and material cost of the war, the painting points to its divisive nature and its future consequences on Irish society. To the artist, the idealism associated with the struggle for independence has been replaced by indifference, disillusionment and personal interest.

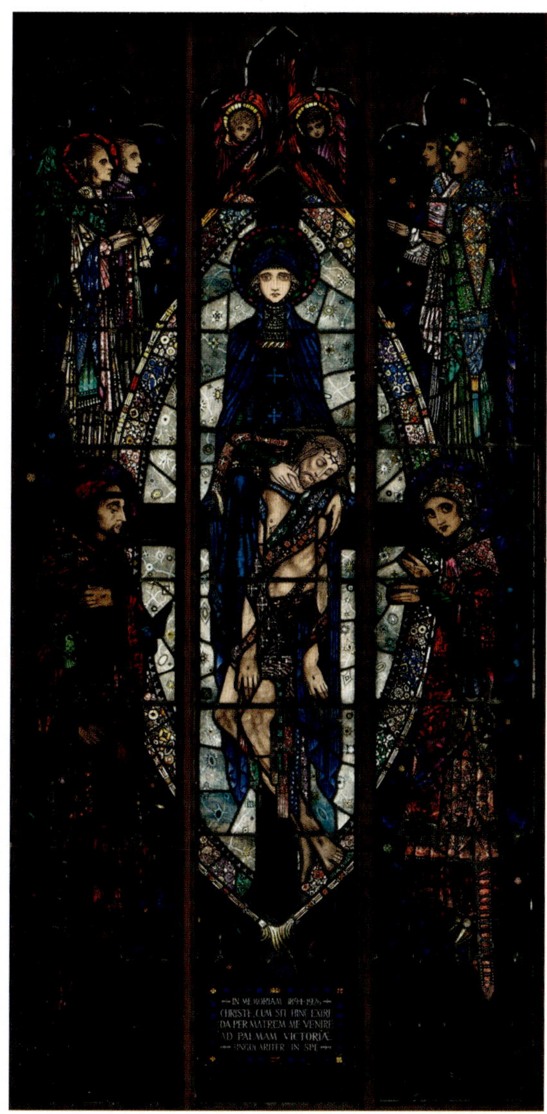

Harry Clarke

Dublin 1889–1931 Coire, Switzerland

The Mother of Sorrows, 1926

Stained glass, 344 x 162 x 13.5 cm
Purchased, 2002
NGI.12262

The subject of Clarke's richly detailed window is a Pietà, with the sorrowful Virgin holding the limp and emaciated body of Christ. Flanking them are St Francis of Assisi, barefoot in a richly painted habit, with birds fluttering around him, and St Catherine of Genoa, one of whose visions was that of the dead Christ being held in the arms of his Mother. St Catherine of Genoa's dress is predominately red, symbolising the fire of Divine Love. Above are angels in prayer. The background sky is ultramarine blue with tiny colour insets that sparkle as they catch the light. The mandorla has a border of tiny bunched flowers and at its centre are various aqueous organisms, suggesting the origins of life.

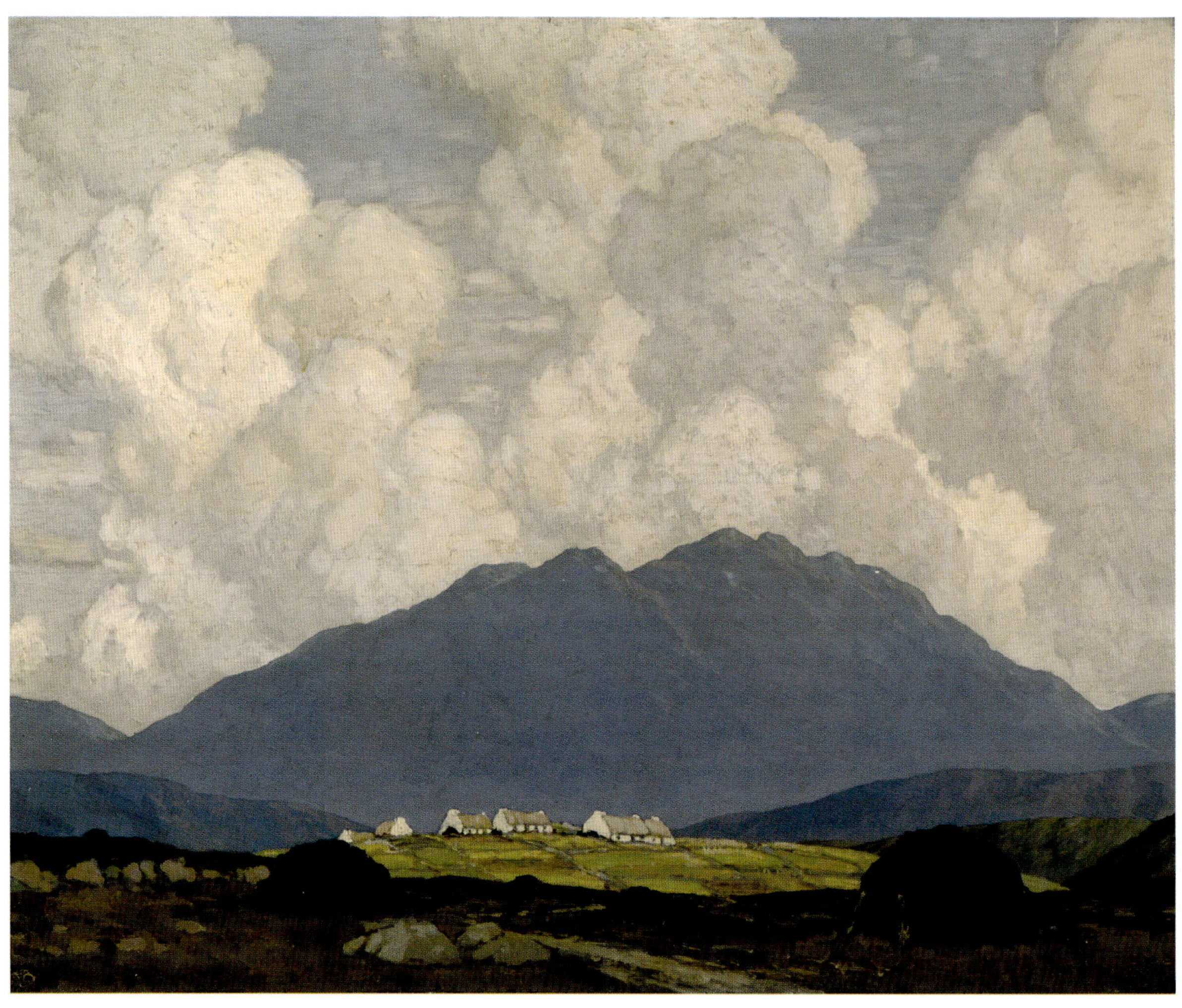

Paul Henry

Belfast 1876–1958 Bray, County Wicklow

A Connemara Village, 1930–1933

Oil on wood panel, 76.2 x 91.4 cm
Purchased, 2004
NGI.4734

This comparatively large painting records with great accuracy the view eastwards from the quay on the Clifden road, just over a kilometre west of Letterfrack, County Galway. The cluster of diminutive cottages, picked out by sunlight against a backdrop of mountains and sky, is a motif that recurs in Henry's landscape painting from the early 1920s onwards. Human activity is conspicuous by its absence. The landscape is animated instead by the interplay of physical elements and profiles, the play of light upon them, and the bold patterns and shapes created by voluminous clouds.

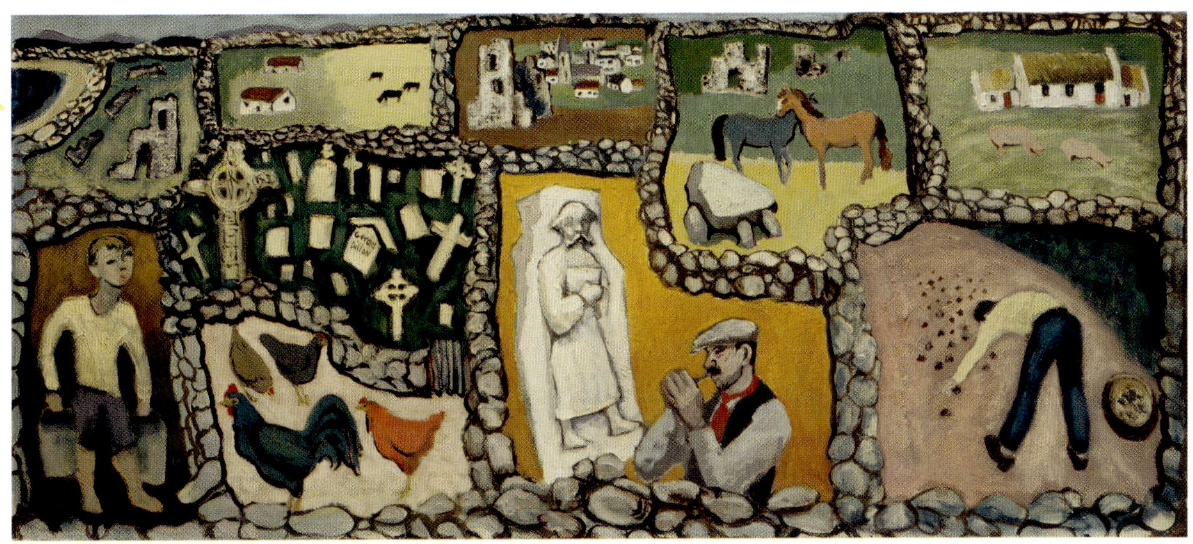

Gerard Dillon

Belfast 1916–1971 Dublin

The Little Green Fields, c.1946–1950

Oil on canvas, 40.5 x 89 cm
Bequeathed, Máire MacNeill Sweeney, 1987
NGI.4520

Dillon made his first of many visits to the west of Ireland in 1939. He was inspired by the rugged and beautiful landscape of Connemara and the simple lifestyle of its inhabitants. In this flat, strongly patterned composition, Dillon brings together motifs associated with the western seaboard and its people: dry-stone walls; thatched cottages; ponies; labour on the land. An old graveyard symbolises both religious devotion and the habitation of the land over generations. A dolmen, a relief sculpture of a monk, the ruins of an abbey, and a high cross, meanwhile, refer to the region's Celtic and early Christian past.

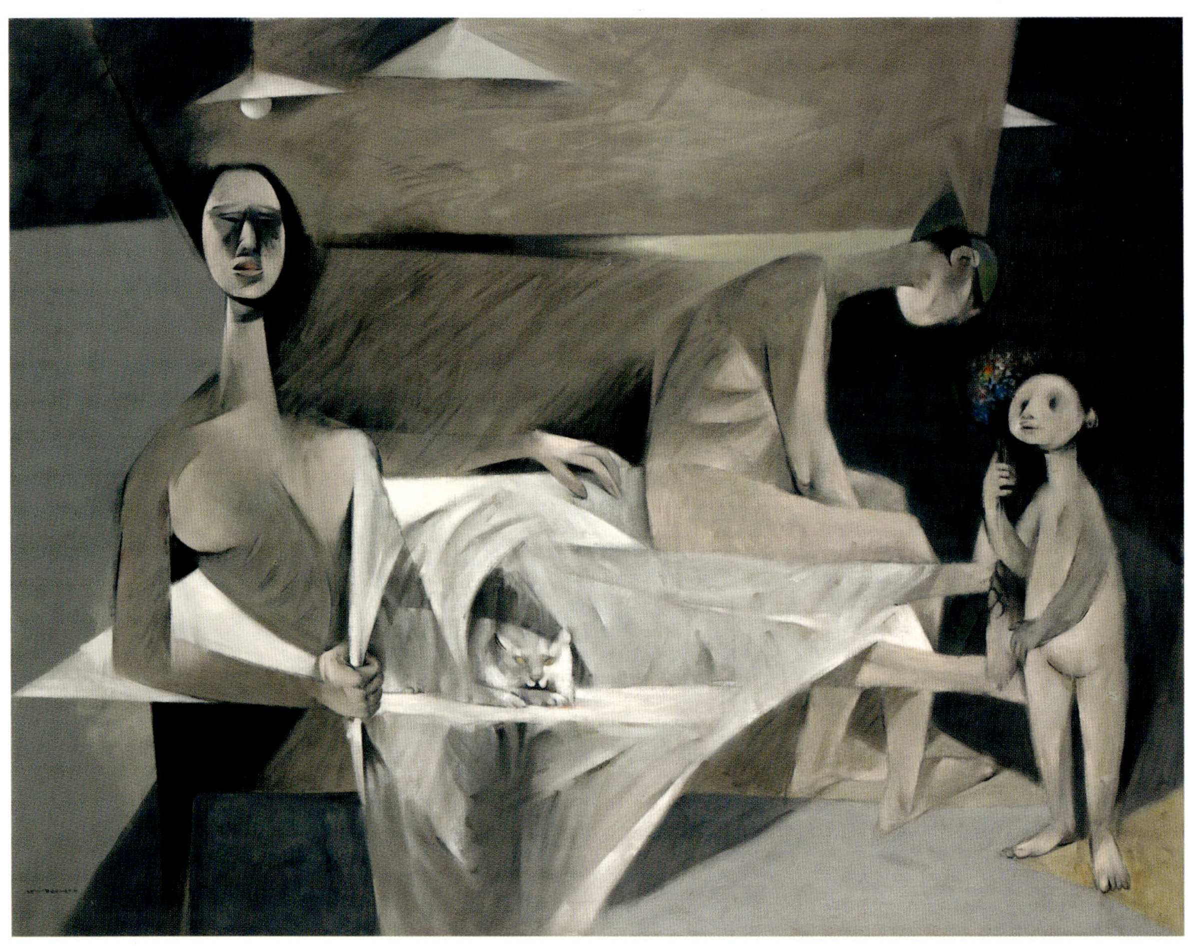

Louis le Brocquy

Dublin, 1916–2012

A Family, 1951

Oil on canvas, 147 x 185 cm
Heritage Gift, Lochlann and Brenda Quinn, 2002
NGI.4709

This is counted among le Brocquy's so-called 'Grey' paintings, characterised by their restricted palette and melancholic tone. Painted in London, where le Brocquy had settled in 1946, the picture was conceived against a backdrop of nuclear threat, widespread social upheaval and the vast refugee crisis that followed the Second World War. The painting calls to mind the work of the Cubists, and Picasso in particular, but also owes a debt to Manet's *Olympia*, which le Brocquy had first seen in Paris in 1938. In his picture, le Brocquy challenges conventional perceptions of both the family and the mother figure.

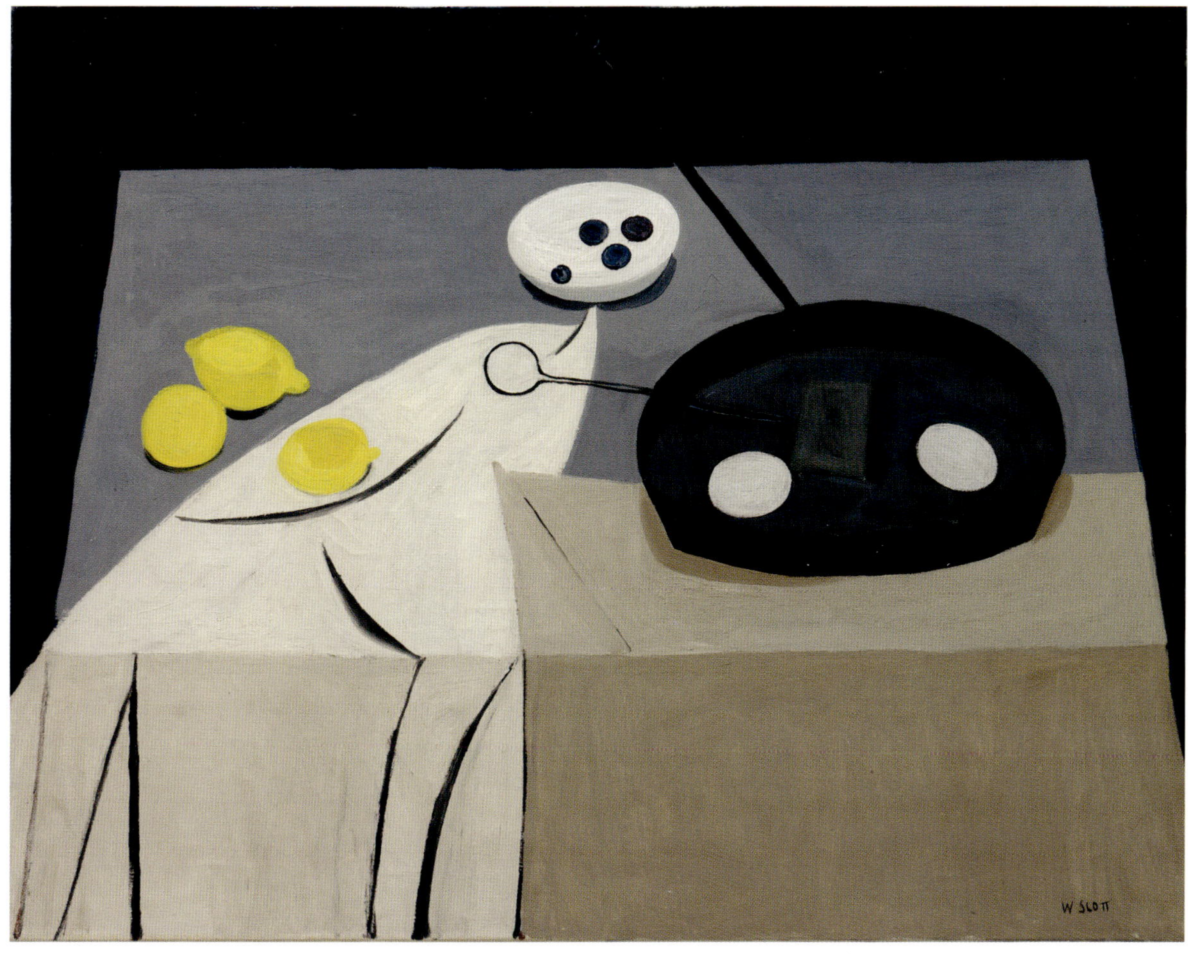

William Scott

Greenock, Scotland 1913–1989
Coleford, Somerset

Frying Pan, Eggs and Napkin, 1950

Oil on canvas, 74 x 91 cm
Purchased, 2010 (Shaw and Dargan Fund)
NGI.2010.5

Scott coupled a fascination with still-life painting with an unusual ability to capture spatial tension through the juxtaposition of simplified, everyday objects. Though he was essentially indifferent to the function of these items, he was acutely aware of their place in the still-life tradition. Scott also possessed a keen eye for colour, as demonstrated by this work, which relies heavily for its impact on the contrast between the blues of the background and the vibrant yellow of the lemons. This contrast complements the interplay between the various elements and shapes of the composition.

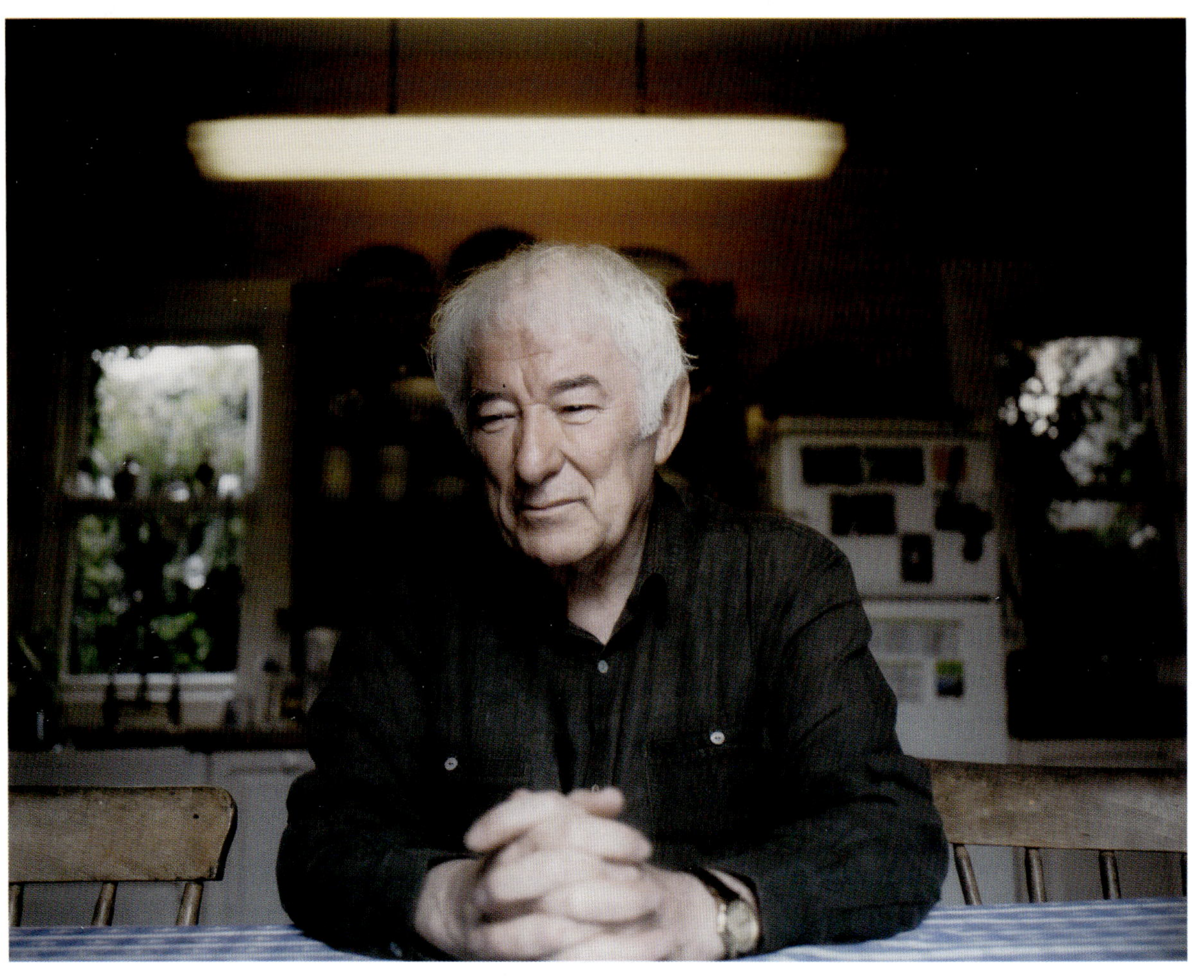

Jackie Nickerson

b. 1960 Boston, Mass.

Seamus Heaney (1939–2013), Poet, Playwright, Translator, Nobel Laureate, 2007

Digital C-print, 52 x 63 cm
Presented, Phoebe Matson and Tom Gurry, 2012
NGI.2012.21

This photographic portrait records the warm, contemplative expression characteristic of the much-loved Irish poet Seamus Heaney. In 2007 Jackie Nickerson was commissioned by a British newspaper to take a photograph of the poet for a feature article. After the formal sitting in his Dublin home, Heaney invited the photographer into the kitchen for a cup of tea where she asked to take another, more informal, shot. The fluorescent light glowing above Heaney's head in the resulting photograph has echoes of a halo.

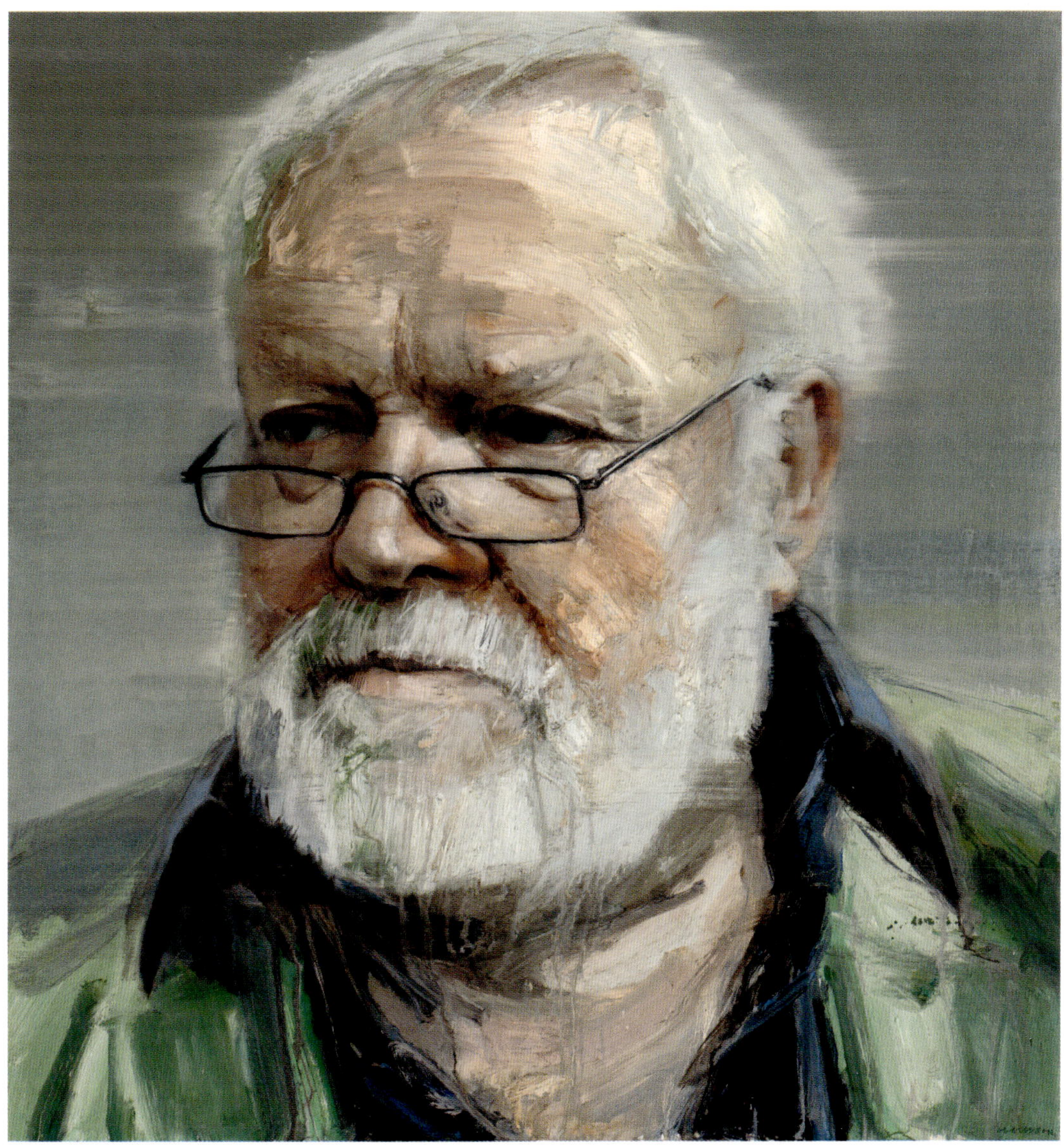

Colin Davidson

b. 1968 Belfast

Portrait of Michael Longley (b. 1939), Poet, Editor and Anthologist, 2011–2012

Oil on linen, 127 x 117 cm
Presented, 2012
NGI.2012.19

This work is one of a series of oversized portrait heads by Davidson of private individuals and public figures. It has been executed with painterly vigour typical of the artist but also a sensitivity that belies its monumental scale. Born in Belfast, Michael Longley is one of Ireland's most celebrated poets, editors and anthologists. He has published more than a dozen collections of poetry, won various prestigious awards and had several public honours conferred upon him. This painting was acquired for the National Portrait Collection, an integral part of the Gallery's permanent collection.

INDEX